FOREVER A PRIEST

How little Audrey Santo and a Eucharistic mystery helped a retired priest get out of his rocking chair and on the road

by Father Thomas McCarthy, C.S.V.
with Cynthia Nicolosi

ISBN# 1 - 891280 - 57 - 0

Library of Congress # 2001012345

Publisher:
CMJ Marian Publishers
and Distributors
Post Office Box 661
Oak Lawn, Illinois 60454
Tel: 708-636-2995 / Fax: 708-636-2855
Toll Free: 1-888-636-6799
http://www.cmjbooks.com
jwby@aol.com

Dedicated to
the Most Holy Sacrament of the Altar
in which is contained
the Body and Blood,
Soul and Divinity
of Our Lord Jesus Christ,
and to all priests who,
by the power of their Sacred Ordination,
celebrate this Mystery daily
in all corners of the world.

The sacrament of orders is so closely associated with the sacraments of the Eucharist and penance that everything pertaining to these unique gifts of Christ to his Church also pertains to the unique powers that only those specially ordained to the priestly office possess.

Yet in our day, as in other significant eras of Catholic Christianity, certain aspects of the priesthood have come under special scrutiny or face extraordinary challenges. In the process of undergoing the reflection and self-understanding that these occasion, the Church has become more aware of what the priesthood really means, and its teaching has taken on a clarity that promises to make this mystery of the faith particularly vital in the years to come.

The Catholic Catechism
John A. Hardon, S.J.

Editor's Preface

On June 5, 1996, seventy-six year old Father Thomas McCarthy was concelebrating Mass in the little chapel of the Santo home in Worcester, Massachusetts. At the moment of the elevation, a small host lying on the paten began to bleed. Father McCarthy witnessed this event with his own eyes. His life would never be the same again.

The truth of the matter is that Father McCarthy's life was already something extraordinary. His vocation first came to him as a fifth grader in a South Boston Catholic school. But God's call would have to wait many years and the purification of many trials to come to fruition. At the age of sixteen, after the departure of his alcoholic father, Tom McCarthy assumed financial responsibility for his mother, seven brothers, and one sister. This was during the Great Depression. After four years of scraping together an existence, he finally found steady work in a shipyard, all the while clinging to the hope that once his family were on their feet he could realize his dream of the priesthood. Just when it seemed like the moment had come, the outbreak of World War II forced him to remain on the job building ships for the war effort. Finally, at the age of twenty-five, a late vocation by the standards of his day, he entered the Clerics of St. Viator in Chicago and started towards the priesthood.

But the road did not get any easier for the young man from Southie. Unprepared for university study, he sweat out every hour of his college and seminary education until, at last, at the age of thirty-two, he was ordained a priest. He then spent twenty years teaching in Catholic high schools and sixteen years serving in parish ministry. At the same time, he managed to fit in twenty-seven years working as a retreat priest for Worldwide Marriage Encounter, Beginnings Experience and Retrouvaille. In later years, he served as hospital chaplain, Knights of Columbus chaplain, director of his order's retirement center, and – to top it off – Irish fiddler.

In a world grown accustomed to bad press about the clergy, Father McCarthy's life stands as a memorial to every unsung, faithful priest – to borrow his own words – "just doing his thing for the Kingdom of God."

Still, skeptics may ask, "That's all very well, but why a book about the man? Isn't the bleeding host the really important thing? Wasn't Father McCarthy just in the right place at the right time? After all, he never founded an order; he never gave a million to charity; he doesn't hold a high office in the ecclesiastical order. Shouldn't we just keep the focus on the bleeding host? Isn't that what it's all about?"

To answer this question, we need to step back from the sensational for a minute and look at the big picture. The Church has always taught that the wondrous acts of God called "miracles" are meant to draw attention to something beyond themselves. They are not detached, isolated events; on the contrary, they are an integral part of God's redemptive plan. Miracles serve to prepare for, nurture, and increase faith. They confirm a message or unveil the true nature of a hidden supernatural reality. The curing spring of water at Lourdes and the miracle of the sun at Fatima are two instances in which miracles served to verify messages and events of supernatural origin. To put it in very graphic terms, a miracle is a kind of "neon sign" pointing to an invisible reality that God wants us to acknowledge in faith.

Unfortunately, the true nature of miracles is often forgotten in our time. Many people are more wrapped up in the "abracadabra" of a mystical manifestation than the vital lesson it imparts. They run around chasing down apparitions and seeking out supernatural phenomena without ever entering into the spirit of prayer and penance that these events invite.

With this said, let's consider again June 5, 1996.

The first thing the bleeding host miracles points to is the Real Presence of Jesus Christ in the Eucharist, the summit and source of Catholic worship (*Catechism* #1324). To those outside the Church, the Eucharist is truly a sign of contradiction. How is it possible that the Eternal God is present under the form of bread and wine? The words of the *Tantum Ergo*, sung for centuries during Benediction, say simply, "Faith supplies where senses fail." Throughout history, when faith was lacking, miracles served to call attention to the Real Presence: mysterious lights, ciboriums or monstrances suspended in the air, and most dramatically, hosts shedding blood – sometimes so profusely as to splatter the walls and pour onto the floor. Wherever these events took place, conversions followed and a wave of Eucharistic devotion expressed itself in pilgrimages and the building of churches.[1]

Yet, a Eucharistic miracle is really a one-two punch: you can't talk about the Eucharist without including the

---

[1] See Joan Carroll Cruz, *Eucharistic Miracles* (Rockford, IL: Tan Books and Publishers, 1991).

priesthood. The Holy Father has written, "Every priest is a hidden force." If a Eucharistic miracle points to the Real Presence of Christ under the outward forms of bread and wine, it also reminds us of the presence of Christ in the priest who pronounces the consecrating words, "This is MY body . . . this is MY blood." Not by accident does the priest speak in the first person. He is, at that moment, *in persona Christi*, acting as Christ by virtue of the sacrament of ordination that he has received.

The mystery of the priesthood is even more heightened if we consider the men who are called to this sacred ministry. They come in all shapes and sizes, personalities and backgrounds, ethnic groupings and political persuasions. The only common denominator among them is the One Priesthood of Christ that they share. Just as faith penetrates the appearances of bread and wine, so does it recognize Christ present in every one of His priests.

Up to this point, the lessons we have drawn could be said of every Eucharistic miracle. But this would be to forget the extraordinary *setting* of the miracle of June 5, 1996. We must place this event within the framework of the amazing supernatural activity happening around little Audrey Santo. We find ourselves standing in front of a great work of Divine art in which every element has something to teach us. What incredible imagery: the tiny, broken body of a semi-comatose girl and the aging, retired priest. Everything about this story is a meditation for our time.

To the naked eye, little Audrey is passivity incarnate. She is in a coma-like condition, completely dependent on the loving care of others. In the estimation of the world, she contributes nothing; her life is without visible fruit. To the eye of faith, however, little Audrey is a hidden force, a "secret weapon" of God. Some have called her a "victim soul", meaning that by her acceptance of her suffering she is a mediator of God's grace in the world. Despite her utterly dependent physical condition, little Audrey is producing fruit in abundance by the power of the Holy Spirit.

How can we have the audacity to make this claim? Because the bleeding host is a Divine ratification, if you will, of what little Audrey is living in secret. Consider the passive nature of the bleeding host miracles in Audrey's home. No host has bled in the hands of a priest at the moment of consecration. On the contrary, three hosts have bled as they lay hidden in the tabernacle. The bleeding host that Father McCarthy witnessed was not the large one used during consecration, but one of the small hosts lying among others in the paten on the altar. Each of these manifestations draws our eyes toward the silent, restful, welcoming presence of Jesus hidden under the form of unleavened bread.

In a similar way, our eyes should be drawn to the reality of the full human life present in little Audrey and all those who are unable to make themselves seen and heard in this world. It's as if God were saying, "Don't stop short at appearances! Recognize my presence in the human *soul*. Recognize the work I am doing in the tabernacle of the human heart." The soul, though unseen, is as much a reality as the physical material it informs. Unfortunately, in our time, the lack of this spiritual vision has made the "out of sight" the "out of mind." We have but to think of the countless unborn humans who are threatened by scientific manipulation or legalized abortion. Surely, we are called to be apostles of the Real Presence not only in the Eucharist but in each human person.

And what of the figure of the aging priest in our portrait? Is it an accident that he is old and retired? Not likely. Father Tom stood on the altar that day at the Santo home, a hidden force just waiting to be revealed. By the grace of God, this is exactly what happened.

The *Catechism* tells us that a priest is marked for all eternity by an "indelible spiritual character" (#1582-1583). This teaching is based on the words of Holy Scripture: "You are a priest forever . . ." (Ps 110:4; Hb 5:5-6, 6:20, 7:24). How, then, can we speak of a priest retiring? A priest is not like a plumber or a teacher. He doesn't just walk out of the office one day and call it quits. He is not merely a professional, but an ontological reality. No matter what his age or condition, he can render the Eternal God present on the altar and restore the Divine image in a soul marred by sin. He is a walking defiance of death, a constant reminder of the eternal life.

Thanks to the visible miracle of the bleeding host, Father McCarthy rediscovered the invisible treasure of his own priesthood. He responded to this grace with his whole heart and became himself a continually unfolding sign of God's power.

In my frequent correspondence with Father McCarthy, I have often had to remind myself that this man is in his eighties. He lives with the enthusiasm and energy of a teenager. He is always learning, always setting challenges for himself, always standing in amazement at the work God is doing in his life and the lives of people around him. He travels all over the country speaking to prayer groups, conferences and retreats, giving his testimony about the bleeding host and blessing the people with the oil collected at little Audrey's home. He has become an apostle of the

Real Presence and a rallying point for the Apostolate of a Silent Soul.

People will first be drawn to this story by the sensational character of the Eucharistic event that happened on that June day in 1996. I hope, though, that the story we are telling will leave something more substantial in the souls of our readers. I hope that the next time you go to Mass in your parish church, in the pew where you always sit, surrounded by the tiny flock you are accustomed to finding around you, you will be more attuned to the man on the altar and the Mystery that he is living and celebrating.

That's what miracles are for.

Cynthia Nicolosi
Editor for CMJ Marian Publishers
August 4, 2003
Feast of St. John Vianney

A Priest Forever

Acknowledgements

I would like to express my gratitude to the many people who have made this book possible, especially Mr. James Gilboy, president of CMJ, for publishing my story, and Cynthia Nicolosi for making these pages come to life. I would also like to remember Gina Friend and the late Harriet Lechleider for encouraging me to get off my rocking chair and start promoting the Real Presence of the Lord in the Holy Eucharist.

I would also like to thank all those who have contributed to the inspiration, writing, and final proofing of this book: Fr. Steve Sotiroff, Debbie Prior, and Vanessa Keck for inviting me to be part of their Marian conference in Vandalia, Illinois, and for their encouragement; Charlotte Fiorillo, who willingly helped me edit my first major speaking engagement at the Du Page mini-Marian conference in November 1997; and Larry and Mary Sue Eck for inviting me to speak at this conference and for publishing my talk in the 1998 spring edition of their Medjugorje magazine. I would also like to thank Connie and Rick Altman and Kevin and Crystal Sullivan for their invaluable advice on the chapter on Marriage Encounter.

Many thanks to friends and members of the St. Viator family: Fr. George Auger, C.S.V., for his proofreading and valuable suggestions; Fr. Patrick Hayes, C.S.V., for his support; Fr. Thomas von Behren. C.S.V., assistant provincial and president of St. Viator High School in Arlington Heights, Illinois, for his help with computer-related questions and the printing of the manuscript; Fr. James Michaletz, C.S.V., for helping me print one of the chapters, and Fr. Donald Fitzsimmons, C.S.V., for sharing some of his computer expertise. I also want to thank Rose Martina, former secretary, and Donna Schwartz, Donna Busse, and Donna Szareck, present secretaries, of our Viatorian provincial offices in Arlington Heights for reading the manuscript and offering their valuable secretarial insights. Thanks also to Adam Clementi for reading the manuscript and helping me with the computer.

I want to extend a special thanks to Fr. Charles Bolser, C.S.V., provincial of the Clerics of St. Viator Chicago Province and the members of the Viatorian Provincial Council for permission to publish this book.

I would also like to mention Brother Don Houde, C.S.V., former Director of Administrative Affairs for Catholic Education of the Archdiocese of Chicago; Fr. Ken Morris, C.S.V., former provincial of the Clerics of St. Viator, Chicago Province; Fr. Dan Nolan, C.S.V., provincial counselor and director of vocations; Fr. Arnold Perham, C.S.V., mathematics department at St. Viator High School in Arlington Heights; and Brother Leo V. Ryan C.S.V., Professor Emeritus, De Paul University, Chicago.

My brother Vincent McCarthy and his wife Ginny were the first ones to encourage me to visit little Audrey Santo. Without their gentle pushing, this story might have had a very different ending. I regret that Ginny passed away as this book was being prepared for publication. May she rest in peace.

I must also give a nod to the Palm Court restaurant in Arlington Heights where Harriet and Gina enthusiastically listened to my account of the bleeding host and then urged me to share my testimony with others. The Palm Court was also the scene of my first meeting with Jim Gilboy the day he expressed his interest in publishing my story.

I would also like to mention some of my good friends at Luther Village in Arlington Heights: Evelyn McDonald, president of Luther Village Spiritual Enrichment Program, Fred and Dorothy Brandstatter, Richard Gaiser, Bea Heimerdinger, Charles Csar, Myrtle O'Hara, Agnes Consadori, Helen Legenza, Marian Moser, Marshall Rowley, Emily Osiol, Virgina Waskowski, Bernice Willard, Joe and Loretta Dobrzycki, Fran De Nardo, Shirley Lownds, Rose Ruddy, and many others.

Last, but not least, I want to thank the Missionary Sisters of the Sacred Heart and Our Lady of Guadalupe for their generosity and support in taking care of my needs, as well as the needs of the Viatorian fathers and brothers at our provincial and retirement centers and the faculty house of St. Viator High School in Arlington Heights.

May the Blessed Virgin Mary, my companion and comfort through all my years, ask Her Son to bless everyone who has been part of my life journey.

Fr. Thomas P. McCarthy, C.S.V.
August 15, 2003
Feast of the Assumption

A Priest Forever

Contents

Chosen to Witness

My trip to Worcester in June 1996 was in most ways like all the others. I didn't expect anything extraordinary to happen – anything, that is, more extraordinary than what was already taking place in the home of little Audrey Santo. I had known little Audrey and her family since 1990 when my brother Vincent and his wife Ginny first introduced me to them. At that time, I was serving as a priest in the South Boston area and, thanks to Vincent and Ginny, had many opportunities to go out to Worcester to see little Audrey and say Mass in the converted one-car garage that her family uses as a chapel. I became very familiar with the mysterious manifestations taking place in the Santo home: the hosts that had bled in the tabernacle, the oil dripping profusely from religious statues and pictures, the signs of the passion on little Audrey's body, and the talk of miraculous healings. Truly, little Audrey had already touched my life as she had touched the lives of so many.

Looking back now, I can see how the hand of Divine Providence arranged for me to be present in little Audrey's home on June 5 that year. I had grown up in South Boston – "Southie," for those who know her and love her. Forty-four

1

years as a priest had carried me far and wide, until I finally landed in my order's retirement center in Arlington Heights near Chicago, Illinois. Still, I made it a point every summer to get back east to see the family and friends I still had there. I was delighted, then, when my brother Paul called inviting me to his daughter Maureen's wedding on the first of June. I decided to go a couple of days early so I could be with the family for the wedding rehearsal and dinner.

Everything about my trip was pleasantly familiar. It's a short flight from Chicago to Boston; as usual, I got on and off easily not having any luggage to check in. I always packed light for these trips since I knew that Celia, the housekeeper at Sts. Peter and Paul rectory, would take care of my laundry. I had served for three years in Sts. Peter and Paul parish and always had a room waiting for me there for these occasional jaunts home. I didn't need to be picked up at the airport since I'm an old hand at getting myself around in Boston. Truth be told, I also like taking the cheap route into the city. With my senior citizen's pass I can ride the subway for twenty cents – maybe not the most glamorous way to travel, but it's faster and cheaper than hiring a cab. What can I say? Fifty-five years living the vow of poverty teaches a man to do with what he has.

The family had a great time with the preliminaries for Maureen's big day and the wedding came off without a hitch on Saturday morning. Sometime during the reception, my brother Vincent worked his way over to me and asked if I wanted to go out to Worcester on the following Wednesday to say Mass at the Santo home. He knew, of course, that my answer would be an enthusiastic "Yes." Even then, we were absolutely of one mind about little Audrey's place in our lives.

After so many years attending these afternoon Masses in Worcester, we all knew the routine. On the morning of June 5th, I got up around 7:00 A.M., had breakfast, and then spent a few minutes with the *Boston Globe*. Right on cue, my brother picked me up at 10:00 A.M. He was driving his new Buick with air conditioning – a necessity for the comfort of his wife Ginny who suffers from emphysema. At that time, she had to be on oxygen at least eight hours a day and carried a tank with her everywhere. As we drove along, we talked about the wedding and other family goings-on. I noticed Ginny breathing on a mouth inhaler to soothe a painful spasm. I really felt for her.

We stopped for lunch at a restaurant in Worcester and then gradually made our way to Christ the King Church where we parked the car and waited for the shuttle that took us directly to the simple, ranch-style house on South Flagg Street. It's funny, the little details you remember later. As we pulled up, I noticed that the light-green grass of the front yard needed cutting. I also saw that the wide garage door on the chapel had been replaced by a normal entranceway. Signs identified the building as the home chapel of little Audrey Santo. Above the door to the right was a plastic crucifix attached to a wooden cross. Several volunteers were standing outside, among whom I immediately recognized Mary Cormier, president of Apostolate for a Silent Soul which at that time was working out of the basement of the Santo home. (Since then they have purchased the house next door.)

I left Vincent and Ginny and joined the small group of priests who had congregated in the main part of the house. Father George Joyce was with us, as usual. He was, at that time, spiritual director for the Santo family and must have been a regular at the Wednesday afternoon Masses because I always found him there during my visits. It was great to see him again with his distinctive dark-rimmed glasses and his watch worn on the right arm. Over the years, I had come to appreciate Father Joyce as a man deeply in love with Christ and totally dedicated to little Audrey.

We priests spoke for awhile, mostly about little Audrey and what the bishop was saying concerning this "shrine" dedicated to a silent soul. Then we moved into the makeshift sacristy where we found our vestments. As usual, I had brought my own alb along. Father Joyce was to be the main celebrant that day, with Father Leo Potvin and I concelebrating. I did not know Father Leo and we did not talk much before Mass. He impressed me by his rather rugged physique and thick gray beard. I also admired his stole with the imprint of the Jerusalem cross in the middle.

As we processed into the chapel, I was surprised to notice a professional camera crew preparing to videotape the Mass. Later, I found out that John Clote, director of the Mercy Foundation of Libertyville, Illinois, had already been with the Santos for five weeks filming little Audrey's life story for a one-hour documentary. Some scenes from the Mass were to be included in this documentary. Little did John Clote realize that his work was about to be blessed in an extraordinary way!

The chapel was packed that day. In addition to the three priests on the altar, the pews were filled with about thirty-five pilgrims representing a mixed bag of people from all over the United States. Two Indian priests, students from Holy Cross, I believe, were also in the congregation. Out of the corner of my eye, I could see that the cameraman had hardly any room to move about. I half-wondered what he was doing there anyway. As the ceremony went on, I could feel the temperature rising with the presence of so many people in such a small space. Mostly, however, I kept my attention on the liturgy and opened myself up to the action of the Holy Spirit. Despite the discomfort of limited space, the atmosphere in the chapel was, as always, a curious combination of tranquility and excitement. I have noticed this energy, this "charge," if you will, during every Mass I have said at little Audrey's home. The presence of so many wonders in little Audrey's chapel keeps you spiritually awake. You know you are on sacred ground, in the presence of something awesome and deep.

The Mass, as usual, was very simple and quiet. No music. No servers. As I had observed on many other occasions, Father Joyce's soul-filled demeanor lent an air of holiness and solemnity to the liturgy. His homily, like always, was a reflection on the holiness of the little girl lying in her bedroom just a few steps away. He also singled out Linda and Steve Santo as attentive and caring parents who have dedicated their lives to letting the whole world know that the Lord is speaking to everyone through the life of their little girl.

After the homily, Mass continued in the usual way through to the consecration. Following the *Lamb of God*, Father Joyce elevated the large consecrated host for all to see before saying the words, "Behold the Lamb of God who takes away the sins of the world." The words did not come. At the very moment he raised the large host, Father Joyce glanced down and saw a spot of dark red on one of the small hosts resting on the paten.

Father Joyce gasped in amazement. He lowered the large host and placed it delicately on the paten. Then, he picked up the tiny bleeding host and showed it to the congregation.

Everyone could see the dark red spot at the center of the host. A hushed wave of "ohs" and "ahs" echoed and re-echoed throughout the chapel. Father Joyce put his finger to his lips to ask the people not to get too excited. There was a hush, but you could have cut the atmosphere with a knife. Some people were crying; others were sobbing quietly.

Standing as I was, so close to the altar, I had a perfect view of everything that was happening. I couldn't believe my eyes. What kind of words can you place on such an experience? Surprised . . . bewildered . . . overwhelmed. Here I was, a humble priest of no great accomplishment or importance, standing in a chapel made from a converted one-car garage, yet witnessing one of the greatest miracles possible. I felt a strange sensation spreading throughout my body – a mix of awe and fear and wonder.

Father Joyce laid the special host aside for the time being. We then had communion and concluded Mass in the usual way. Later, the bleeding host was placed with the others in the tabernacle of little Audrey's bedroom.

Immediately after the Mass, John Clote was on the spot with his camera to interview Father Joyce and me. He did so right there in the chapel. (For some reason Father Leo was not interviewed. He left immediately after Mass and I have not seen or heard from him since that day.) When John asked me what I was feeling, I couldn't find words at first. I felt like Peter at the transfiguration, babbling because the event was too big for him. Somehow I pulled myself together and said, "I was flabbergasted. I did not know what to say. I did not know what to do. I did know a miracle was taking place." I also tried to express to John how unworthy I felt to be witness to such a manifestation of Christ's presence on the altar; though at the same time, I accepted that God in his goodness had chosen Father Joyce, Father Leo, and me. The two student priests from India who were present in the congregation concurred with me that this was a wonderful expression of God's love for each one of us priests and pilgrims.

With all the interviewing done, the groups of us remaining after the Mass were like the apostles on Mount Tabor, wanting to linger and continue drinking in the mystery that we had experienced. The ordinary necessities of life, however, meant we each had to go our own way. Ginny only had so much oxygen in her tank and we still had plans to eat out before getting home. I just had time to exchange a few words with Linda Santo before departing. We rejoiced in the miracle[2] we had just witnessed together and I expressed my hope to see them all again soon.

On our drive back to Boston, all we could do was talk about the great event that had happened that day. We went over the story again and again, recalling every detail and describing every feeling. I was on cloud nine – so charged up with emotion that I couldn't tell you if it was rainy or sunny out. Ginny and Vincent were happy that the cameraman had focused on the both of them for a few seconds. (In fact, they appear briefly in the Mercy Foundation video.) The conversation kept up its momentum as we stopped for dinner at the "L" Street fisheries in South Boston. We were like children celebrating Christmas in June, immersed in festive joy.

---

[2] I want to qualify my use of the word miracle here and in other places in this book. No event can be considered an actual miracle until the Church says so. Those of us who witnessed the bleeding host that day, as well as the many other mysterious manifestations which happen in the Santo home, use the word "miracle" in an informal and subjective sense.

Back again at the rectory, I tried to absorb all that happened to me that afternoon. The knowledge that God had chosen me specially to witness the bleeding host had me hovering between fear and rejoicing. Awe at His majesty and gratitude for His love swelled my heart. For the first time, I understood something about how Moses must have felt as the voice of Almighty God spoke to him on Mount Sinai. I could share something with Elizabeth when she asked, "Who am I that the mother of my Lord should come to me?" or the Centurion when he stated simply, "Lord, I am not worthy..."

I have to say that apart from my priestly ordination, June 5, 1996, was the most moving day of my life. As a priest, I experience the changing of the bread and wine into the Body and Blood of Christ at every Mass; but on that day, God blessed me with a special confirmation of the reality of Christ's sacrificial offering in the Mass. What I had lived in faith had now been confirmed by the testimony of my own eyes. I knew that I would never be the same again.

I couldn't have guessed it at the time, but my life was about to take a radical new direction. I had the first prophetic hints of this "new assignment" the very next day at the 12:10 P.M Mass at Sts. Peter and Paul rectory. During the homily, I told the people about the bleeding host. I gave my first public witness to what I had seen. The congregation responded with amazement and wonder. They wanted to go and experience for themselves the mysteries surrounding little Audrey. For my part, I felt an extraordinary inner peace as I related my experience. I felt I was connecting with my people, touching their hearts with my story and helping them see the Eucharist in a totally new way.

I soon returned home to the retirement center in Arlington Heights, Illinois. Though I spoke to people from time to time about my experience, I did not yet fully understand what God meant to do with my testimony. I returned to my usual routine as a retired priest: bowling, playing a little fiddle, taking the occasional assignment to sub for a priest on leave, and coping with the aches and pains of getting old. Though on the surface no one would have noticed anything different, my interior life was marked by a sense of urgency. I went about my business as though I carried a great secret inside just bursting to come out. This period was like the quiet that surrounds a seed in the earth. All was to unfold in its proper way and time.

In my heart I continued to ponder what I had seen. I could not help asking myself, "Why me?" So many priests – better men than me – would have loved to be in my shoes the moment I witnessed the bleeding host. Why did God reserve this special grace for me? I would never have considered myself the "type" to witness such a great miracle. I'm not very holy. I'm not a mendicant wandering about in poverty begging for alms or a monk leading an austere life of prayer and fasting. I am just a plain, simple priest trying to do his thing for the Kingdom of God.

As far as I could see, there wasn't much in my past that could explain the great gift of the bleeding host, either. I grew up in poverty stricken Irish tenements in South Boston. As a child, I never excelled at anything. I was a mediocre student. I never could boast of very good health. I learned to play a little fiddle. My vocation was what I like to describe as "delayed" since I had to take care of my family after my alcoholic father abandoned us. I struggled through every minute of my seminary studies. I then spent my priesthood doing ordinary things: teaching, parish ministry, giving retreats – nothing sensational. I never founded an order or built a cathedral or preached a crusade. Yet, here I was, chosen from among so many more likely candidates to witness what might have been the first fully documented bleeding host miracle in the history of the United States. It just didn't add up.

I brought my questioning to God in prayer. Why me, Lord? Was there something hidden in my seventy-six years of life, my forty-four years of priesthood, which could explain so wonderful a gift?

**Part I
God Calls a "Southie"
(1920-1945)**

A Priest Forever

Boston Born and Bred

My mother, Rose E. McKernan, was born on November 28, 1896, in the town of Newbliss just a bit east of Upper Lake Erne in the border county of Monaghan, Ireland. For a while, she skirted with the notion of becoming a nun but finally opted for an adventure overseas. She was about eighteen when she left for the United States. Her sister Maggie was born in Ireland after her departure. Fifty years later, the sisters saw each other for the first time when my Uncle Pete and his wife took my mother with them on their summer trip to Ireland.

My father was Thomas P. McCarthy, born in Skibereen, County Cork, in 1892. I don't know what made him leave Ireland, but I imagine he found passage on one of the great Atlantic ocean liners that left from Cobh, the last view of home for thousands of Irish immigrants, as well as the final port of call for the *Titanic*.

Like many Irish immigrants before them, Rose and Thomas settled in Lawrence, Massachusetts, where life revolved around the textile mills. They met and fell in love at the mill where they worked together and were married in St. Mary's Church in Lawrence on July 30, 1918. When the clothing mills went south seeking cheaper labor, my parents went to Boston looking for work and a place to raise their family.

I made my entry into the world in Jamaica Plain, Massachusetts, on May 12, 1920, in the same town where James Michael Curley had been born. He was the famous Boston mayor who once ran the city from a federal prison and whose story became the basis of the book and film *The Last Hurrah*. Tough act to follow. I was the second of eleven children, nine boys and two girls. My parents' first child, little Rose, died in infancy.

The Horans were my parents' closest friends in Jamaica Plain. I could even call them foster parents, we saw so much of them. I can remember my father and Jim Horan, my godfather, making beer in the bathtub – nothing to complain about in itself, but then they had to stay up all night tasting it. By morning my father would be in a drunken stupor. It sounds funny, but it was no laughing matter for my family and a fearful omen for our future.

Just after I completed fourth grade, my family moved to 68 "A" Street in South Boston. That's where I did my real growing up. The area is affectionately known as "Southie," a word also used to designate its residents. Southie is essentially a peninsula suburb of Boston with the harbor on one side and the Fort Point Channel on the other. Broadway runs along the length of the peninsula and ends at City Point where you have a beautiful view of the harbor entrance. In my time, during the day and into the evening, you could see small craft of all kinds and visiting vacation pleasure steamers going back and forth between the city of Boston and the harbor light that guided ships into the harbor. It's much the same way today.

My family landed in a tenement house on the "Lower End," so called to distinguish it from the "East End" of the peninsula. The demographics have changed quite a bit since I was a boy, but I still remember them well. In those days, the East End was for the wealthy, while the Lower End belonged, for the most part, to lower income families. Letters of the alphabet in ascending order from "A" to "P" designated street names from the poorer to the wealthier neighborhoods. You had to get to at least "G" Street to enter the more middle class section of South Boston. Traveling east to "P" Street, you came to what some of us affectionately called the "lace curtain" Irish area. The "G" Street section of East Broadway going toward "H" Street was called "pill hill" because of the number of medical and dental offices found there. Going south two blocks along "G" Street, you came to Dorchester Heights, made famous by George Washington and his troops when they drove the British out of Boston Harbor. South Bostonians commemorate this event as "Evacuation Day," but since it falls on March 17, it gets lost in the St. Patrick's Day festivities.

My father worked as a maintenance engineer for a large factory in the Boston area. Although he had only an elementary education, he was able to keep the fires burning during cold New England days and nights. His only difficulty was that he had a drinking problem and was unable to keep that job, or any other, for any length of time. At one point we had to move bag and baggage to Athol in western Massachusetts because my father had found a job there. This didn't last either. Our short stay in Athol was also accompanied by sorrow. My younger brother John died of blood poisoning.

One good memory I have of Athol is that we felt safe there. In the tenement houses in South Boston, we were always afraid. Those were the days when bootlegging and organized crime were in full swing, especially in the urban areas. We lived in a climate of fear, expecting danger around every corner. Though my family only lived in Athol for a brief time, I remember noticing the difference in atmosphere. For the first time, and for the only time thereafter, I knew what it was like to go outside without caution. I remember, in particular, enjoying Halloween because we could roam freely around the neighborhood begging for candy. Everyone was so kind to us and made a big deal over our costumes. These idyllic days came to an end all too soon.

It isn't easy looking back on my boyhood years. To tell the truth, I'd rather forget them entirely. They are pretty horrifying – like a page out of Frank McCourt's book *Angela's Ashes*. My childhood memories are filled with poverty, embarrassment, and lack of proper food and clothing. We lived on the third floor of a tenement building and, of course, we all had to sleep two or more to a bed. I can remember sitting down to a table of hot tea and day-old bread, our main meal on many occasions. I remember my brothers and I taking our four-wheel red cart on a two-mile trip down "A" Street to get the unburned coke located on a pile outside a large factory. It was humiliating, but necessary, since we didn't have the money to buy coal for the furnace during the cold winter weather in South Boston.

I was not a strong child. When I was about eleven or twelve, I contracted scarlet fever and the Board of Health paid us a visit. They put a sign on the door reading, "Keep out – contagious disease." I was a prisoner in my own home. Since the doctors couldn't cure me, they suggested that I go to Boston City Hospital. I was there for six months. My mother came to see me as often as she could though she didn't have a car and couldn't afford a taxi. It was too far to walk, so she made use of public transportation during rush hour – no easy feat in Boston, even back then. One day, she arrived in my room to find a sign at the foot of my bed reading "DL." She asked the nurses to explain and they told her that the sign meant I was on the danger list. Basically, the doctors had given up hope. I was dying.

My mother scooped me up in her arms and carried me out of the room despite the protests of the nurses. She must have been a very strong woman to carry me out of the hospital, from bus to bus, and then up the three flights of stairs in our tenement building, but she did it. My mother was pretty stubborn. She didn't care what the doctors said. She was going to cure me. She had already lost little Rose and John and she was not about to lose her first-born son, also. She wasn't going to let me go without a fight. I'm not sure if it was the TLC or the homemade custard, but whatever she did, it worked. I recovered from scarlet fever, though it left me with runny ears and perforated eardrums.

Though there was nothing we could do about perforated eardrums, runny ears called for some kind of treatment. We tried everything the doctors suggested and nothing worked. Finally, Mom decided to ask God for a miracle. She took me to the famous mission church in Roxbury, Massachusetts, the Basilica of Our Lady of Perpetual Help, operated by the Redemptorist Fathers. A novena was held there every Wednesday from 5:30 P.M. to 8:00 P.M. As a child, I was awed by the sight of all the crutches left in the sanctuary by those who had been cured at the church.[3] Every week, my mother brought me to Roxbury to attend the Mother of Perpetual Help Novena. No matter what the weather – rain, snow, sleet – just like the mail, we got through. My mother's faith was rewarded. My ears stopped running, although I still had the perforated eardrums.

Being somewhat of a weakling, I was a target for bullying and took a lot of abuse. I remember one time I was playing touch football and some kid challenged me. I immediately ran away. I hated any kind of conflict. That's probably why I never really got into contact sports. There was one instance, however, when I did defend myself. A boy about my size started beating on me for no apparent reason. I stood my ground and punched him back a few times until he decided to leave me alone. I was pretty proud of myself. I bragged about the story and showed off my bruised fists to everyone I met.

There were no playing fields or baseball diamonds near where we lived. Nor could any of us afford sports equipment. We had to be inventive. We used to play a game called "kick the bar" behind a chocolate factory on West Broadway. We had two opposing teams, three bases and an infield and outfield. The person who was up would kick the bar as far as he could. If it was caught in the air, he was out immediately; if it landed on the ground, he could run to first base; if the bar was thrown to the first baseman before the runner crossed first base, he was out. When the side that was up had three outs then the other side would get up. We did

---

[3] The basilica still houses countless crutches attesting to the many miracles that have taken place there. Nowadays, Father Ed McDonough, C.SS.R., celebrates special healing Masses there every last Sunday of the month at 2:00 P.M.

not need an umpire. We usually played about seven innings and the team that had most players cross home plate would win. Sounds a lot like baseball, doesn't it? Minus the ball, the bat, and the gloves, that is.

Finding a place to play had its challenges. The nearest playground was up near the Carson Beach area, quite a long walk. Sometimes our attempts to find a playing area ended in tragedy. I remember one boy lost a leg up to the knee while playing around an elevator shaft on "A" Street where a lot of commercial buildings were located. Swimming was a little easier. The Fort Point Channel was within walking distance. We would jump into the channel from the Broadway Street Bridge that joined South Boston to the rest of the city.

An unlikely but gratifying bit of fun could be had from visiting the homes of the deceased. In those days, there were no funeral parlors. Wakes were held at home. A purple wreath was hung on the door to let people know that the house was open to receive friends and relatives. People would come and go freely to console the family and take a last look at the dearly departed. My friends and I scouted the neighborhood for these purple wreaths. We would then go into the house of mourning, making sure to take our caps off respectfully as we crossed the threshold. (We youngsters in those days always wore caps because that was what Irish men did and we wanted to imitate our elders.) We would pay our respects to the deceased by kneeling in front of the casket and saying some prayers. Then, we would shake hands with the people standing nearby and offer our condolences. Finally, we would help ourselves to the refreshments available, this being the principle reason for our visit.

Of course, no funeral wake was like an Irish funeral wake. As my gang and I moved into late adolescence, we kept our eyes pealed for those purple wreaths in an Irish neighborhood. For one thing, you generally found a woman there who had been hired to cry – professional wailers. For another thing, you could count on finding an ample supply of beer. An Irish wake without Guinness Stout was unheard of. If we minded our p's and q's, nobody stopped to ask us if we were of legal age. We had a great time putting away a good amount of lather, especially since we knew we would never have been served in the local taverns.

Up until Mom's move to Gates Street in St. Augustine's parish, all of us McCarthy children attended Sts. Peter and Paul Elementary School run by the Notre Dame de Namur nuns. Sts. Peter and Paul Church lay in the area between Broadway Station and "A" Street and the parish school was right across the street. This was the parish where I made my First Communion and Confirmation, and where I first felt the stirrings of a vocation to the priesthood.

Founded in 1884, Sts. Peter and Paul was one of the oldest churches in Boston and the first Roman Catholic parish in South Boston. Its Gothic tower stood as a welcoming beacon to wave after wave of immigrants in the 19th and early 20th centuries, the majority of whom arrived from Ireland. The church was an imposing structure made with huge stone boulders about three by five each. Thanks to the surrounding tenement houses, the parish numbered over 10,000 members. The church building was large enough to accommodate them with sanctuaries upstairs and downstairs. I can remember the days when there were two 9:00 A.M. Masses going on at the same time. Sadly, a radical change in demographics in the seventies reduced the number of parishioners to such a point that the church had to be closed.

All the sisters who ran our school were very good to us, but two in particular really influenced me. One was Sister Catherine Veronica whom we all nicknamed "Tarzan" because she was so big and tall. She was a gentle giant, though, and really tried to help us in every way. We used to irritate her when we asked to go to the restroom during class. She would plead with us, "Can't you hold it in? You can hold it in when you are at a movie. Why do you have to interrupt class?" We all loved her. Then there was Sister Anna, the porter of the convent that was part of the school complex. She took a liking to me and was constantly having me do little things around the convent. She always rewarded me with candy or home-baked cookies. That was great, but I suspect that my lifelong dental problems date from Sister Anna's goodies.

Sad to say, not all our teachers at Notre Dame were so nice. The eighth grade lay teacher whacked our hands with a ruler whenever we got out of line. I don't remember committing any really serious infractions, but there were plenty of little misdemeanors that sent me to the front of the class for a hand whacking.

One day, during my fifth grade year, a lady came into the classroom and asked if anyone was interested in learning the violin. I put up my hand. I don't know what motivated me to do this – maybe it was just the McKernan blood stirring in me. My Uncles Frank and Pete were both brilliant Irish musicians. Years later, as an adult, I had the chance to see them together at a family reunion in Ireland. Music just poured out of them until the wee hours of the morning. For my own part, I have to say I am glad I raised my hand that day in class. I began a long and happy relationship with the violin, as well as my teacher Katherine Sullivan. My father was proud of me for the bit of playing I did as a child and liked to have me perform for guests.

I can't say I was a particularly holy little lad. Confession for me during my elementary school days was "a little good news, a little bad news." The good news was that we could get out of class for an hour or so to go to confession. The bad news was that we were herded into the pews where we waited anxiously for our turn in the confessional box. The nuns strongly impressed on us the importance of examining our consciences and confessing all our sins. With a great deal of trepidation and shaking knees, we entered the shadows of the confessional and waited in the dark for the sound of the sliding door opening. Some of the priests were very kind and deeply concerned about our becoming better Catholics. Some were not so. Sometimes on the outside you would hear an exasperated, "You did what?" or "How could you do that?" With that, some of us would try to slide into another line to escape a "mean" confessor. You had the feeling the wrath of God was waiting for you in that box.

I first experienced my vocation to the priesthood when I was in the fifth grade. The associate pastor came into the classroom one day to ask for volunteers to serve at Mass. I immediately raised my hand. I suspect that I was motivated by my natural tendency to be a "helper." This man needed help, and I responded to his need. I'm glad I did. From the first day I served Mass, my future course was set. As I looked up at the priest saying the Mass and then out at the people straining their ears to hear him, I said to myself, "That is where I want to be."

Another little incident that carried me towards the priesthood occurred at the home of my violin teacher, Katherine Sullivan. One day, as I waited my turn for my lesson, an old priest, Father Fitzsimmons, was there working with Katherine. She was playing for him so that he could sing some hymns he was trying to memorize. I was inspired by this elderly priest who would take time out of his busy schedule to learn how to sing better so that he could make the Eucharistic Liturgy more meaningful for his parishioners. I'm sure he couldn't have imagined that he had touched the young lad in the room next door so profoundly, but his example left me with the desire to be a dedicated priest like him.

The years from fifth to eighth grade were happy ones for me since I was up on the altar and near the Lord – right where I wanted to be. Despite some difficulties at home, I was happy and close to my Heavenly Father. I felt He was looking out for me and that we understood each other. He wanted me to be a priest, and I agreed. As the years went by, the priesthood became my only ambition. Nothing else mattered. I was constantly looking toward that day when I could begin fulfilling my mind-boggling vocation of being a priest of God. Until then, I had the consolation and joy of serving at the Mass.

My beautiful dream came to a sudden and painful end in my eighth grade year. The pastor called us servers in and told us that we were no longer needed. He wanted to concentrate on the boys who were still in grammar school. I was crushed. I felt like the rug had been pulled out from under my feet. What was I going to do now? Where was I going to go? What was going to happen to my dream? There was no other way for me to be close to the altar than serving at the liturgy. From that point on, although I went to Mass every Sunday, I had no other relationship with the church. During the trying days ahead, when I really needed help, I turned to the priests of the parish, but they were too busy for me. I felt like an outsider, and I couldn't see how that would ever change. I said to myself, "That's that."

To make matters worse, I knew the archdiocesan seminary in Boston would not accept me because I wasn't going to attend the prestigious Boston College High School. My family just wasn't in that income bracket, and I certainly didn't have the smarts to get in on my own merit. After elementary school, I went to English High School, a public school.

The final blow to my dream came in the second semester of my sophomore year of high school when my father abandoned us. He had begun to drink heavily, and this, coupled with his abusive behavior, was enough to warrant getting him out of the house. I didn't understand at the time that my father was an alcoholic. I only knew that he was hurting my mother. Friday nights were a nightmare. He would beat her up, and if I got in the way to protect her, I got it, too. I can remember one incident when my mother and father were having a loud confrontation and I moved between them to protect my mother. My dad hit me and drove me to the other side of the room. It would be years before I could forgive him.

Being a strong Catholic, my mother did not want to get a divorce, though she eventually sued for legal separation. My father left our home and never returned – not even to say "hello" or see how we were doing. My other brothers and sister, like myself, just learned to get along without our father in our lives. He ended up living in the skid row section of Boston near the Catholic cathedral and eventually died there at the age of eighty-two.

Maybe the responsibility of such a large family was just too much for my father. By the time he left us we were nine children: me (1920), Jim (1921), Vincent (1922), Francis (1924), Charlie (1927), Theresa (1928), Alfred (1929), Paul (1931), Richard (1935) – plus my mother. Ten people to support. Since the tendency to drink was already there, maybe my father just finally caved in like a building with a faulty foundation.

The last straw for my father was the birth of my sister Terry on July 4, 1928. Apparently, he was disappointed because his seventh child was not a boy. According to Irish tradition, the seventh boy is a very special child. My father could never accept or forgive Terry for not being a boy. He went on a drinking binge that never seemed to let up after that point. Maybe it was just a good excuse to let it all go. This kind of thinking certainly seems pretty strange today, though a letter from an old family friend, Mary Wheeler Antinarelli, gave me some insights into how serious it was for my father:

> We were just little ones when my mother and your mother became very dear friends. They were like two sisters, as they became midwives for each other. My mother loved my dad and so did your mother love your dad . . . When your sister was born, as she was the seventh child, your father was so disappointed because he wanted a seventh son. He put your sister Teresa in my arms . . . your mother and father had problems from then on. My mother and father felt so sad for your dear mother and, of course, that was when he started to drink heavy.

On the financial level, my father's departure was catastrophic for the family. To my knowledge, he never sent us any money. We were forced to go on welfare in order to survive, but that still wasn't enough for such a large family. The brunt of the responsibility ended up falling on me, the oldest son. I was forced to leave high school and get a job. No red carpet greeted me as I beat the pavement looking for work. On the contrary, I found the world to be a hostile environment where I was abandoned to the wolves. For one thing, the country was in the middle of the depression and work was hard to come by. For another, many places in Boston with *Help Wanted* signs in the window had another sign right next to it reading, "Catholics and Irish need not apply." With an incomplete education and no talents to speak of, I went from one menial job to another. I washed dishes at a restaurant, served coffee at the old Copley Plaza Hotel, and ran telegrams from the telegraph office to downtown Boston.

There aren't words for what my father's abandonment meant for me. Needless to say, whatever hopes I had for becoming a priest all but died. My life was no longer my own. At the age of sixteen, I was forced to assume the role of father and provider for my family.

Even deeper, on the personal level, I felt my father's absence keenly. I missed the relationship that should exist between a son and his father. He never took me fishing. He never took me to a baseball game. He wasn't there to teach me about life. I needed him to help me learn how to study, to take me on a stroll through the woods and teach me how to identify different birds and animals, to help me understand people and my place in the world – normal things that any boy growing up needs to know. How else was I supposed to know? My mother, God bless her, did not have time to take me aside and teach me about life. She was too busy keeping us alive, with three meals a day to cook and the laundry of ten people to do, in addition to the regular housework – all of this without the support of her husband.

Gradually, I grew to hate my father. I hated him because he did not fulfill his responsibilities to me as his son. I hated him for what he had done to my mother. Maybe I couldn't be blamed for feeling the way I did, but holding on to this hatred prevented me from growing into a whole person. It made it difficult for me to form loving relationships. I couldn't trust anyone. I kept to myself and became a loner. I grew into the habit of doing things, as Frank Sinatra sang, "my way." It would take me many years to emerge from the barriers I had built around my own heart.

The next ten years were the most painful of my life. They were sad, depressing, and in my opinion at the time, wasted years. I felt myself becoming more and more resentful. In essence, I felt abandoned by both of my fathers – the one on earth and the one in heaven. I grew bitter against God. Where was He now when I really needed Him? Why wasn't He taking care of me? Didn't He want me to be a priest? Had it all been a terrible illusion on my part? In my loneliness and pain, I didn't realize that God was there all the time, answering my deepest desires, preparing me for the future He had promised. Everything that was happening in my life was shaping me into the man and the priest He wanted me to be. But I didn't know that at the time. I only knew that I was all alone with a burden too heavy for me to carry, in a world where I could expect neither help nor sympathy.

One night, after coming home from the restaurant where I was working as a dishwasher, I noticed my arm was turning black and blue. I wasn't going to do anything about it, but my mother insisted that I go up to the Carney Hospital Emergency Room, a short distance away from our tenement house. It was a good thing I went when I did because I found out that I had blood poisoning. The nurses immediately started applying compresses to keep the bad blood from getting to my heart and killing me. It had been a close call, and all the more poignant for my family in light of the death of my brother John to the same ailment just a few years before.

While I was being treated for blood poisoning, a doctor's examination also revealed that I had serious problems with my teeth. Not only were my teeth riddled with decay, I also had failed to get a plate when I needed one with the result that the upper teeth on the right side eventually pulled away from the gums. This may sound incredible given the health education standards of today, but no one had ever told me about cleaning my teeth, nor had I ever seen a dentist. Whereas schools these days ensure students receive regular medical exams, I don't remember ever having a dentist look at my teeth. Only after I entered the Viatorian community did I have the opportunity to get proper dental care, but by then it was too late to help much.

After four years doing odd jobs and just barely making ends meet, I finally landed a good position with good pay at the Bethlehem Steel shipyard in Quincy, Massachusetts. I was twenty years old.

Although my dream of being a priest had suffered a severe setback with the departure of my father, I kept it in the back of my mind and did what I could to prepare for the future. One thing was essential: somehow, I needed to complete my high school education. So, while working full time for the shipyard, I continued my studies at Lincoln Preparatory Evening School located near Northeastern University in Boston. This wasn't the easiest way to do things, but it was the only way open to me. It also served to keep burning the small flame of hope in my heart. The day I finally got my high school diploma, I made my peace with God. I realized that He was really taking care of me. I began to trust Him again.

Work and school was a heavy load, but I wasn't the only one with a full schedule. Mom had her hands full taking care of the nine of us. She washed our clothes with a machine that she kept in the already crowded kitchen. When the washer had gone through its cycle she would then place the clothes in a wringer that was attached to it. This was all done by hand. She fed the wet clothes from the washing machine into the wringer while I helped her pump the handle that turned the rollers. Then, she had to hang the clothes on the line that stretched from the kitchen windowsill to the nearest poll in the backyard. The outside line was on rollers so that she could put out a small number of clothes at one time. I can still see her there at the kitchen window clamping the clothes on the line with her left hand while at the same time holding two or more wooden pins in her mouth while she maneuvered the clothesline back and forth. It was like watching the famous violinist Fritz Kreisler flying his fingers up and down the strings playing Paganini's *Perpetual Motion*. Then she had to iron the shirts of nine children. In between, there were three meals a day to put on the table and the regular housecleaning. Back breaking work. I don't know how she did it, but she did. The rest of us had our chores to do, too, but like all kids our age, we tried to get out of them as often as possible. We had our share of fights every night about whose turn it was to do the dishes. Since I was the man of the house after my father left, I was theoretically exempt from doing the dishes – but I did them anyway!

With all the work to do, my mother still managed to be a maternal presence for us. At five feet, four inches tall and heavyset, she was a strong, good-looking woman. She had auburn hair, a well-rounded face and blue eyes. She had a certain local reputation among medical professionals for her skillful home remedies. She had to be inventive because she did not have the money to take us to a doctor. Those times when Mom had to call for medical help, during my bout with scarlet fever, for example, she promised that she would pay somehow. That usually meant knitting an afghan for the doctor. She also gave afghans to many of the priests at St. Augustine's parish in South Boston. My mother was a devout Catholic and a lively participant in her parish and community. When she died, there were at least six priests present for her funeral Mass.

Our house was in many ways typical of the time. My sister Terry remembers coming home from St. Augustine's school to find Mom in a nice, starched dress, doing the ironing, and listening to her favorite programs on the radio. Some of these were the original soap operas. Of course, the radio was a big part of our family life, as it was for everyone in those days. Every weekend we used to listen to *The Shadow* together. "Who knows what evil lurks in the hearts of men? Only the Shadow knows . . ." It sure was a scary show.

On December 7, 1940, the Japanese bombed Pearl Harbor and the United States entered World War II. If I had had any notions of pursuing my dream now that my brothers were entering adulthood, I had to place everything on hold again to answer the call of my country. My work at the shipyard was considered necessary for the war effort. I was frozen to my job. I did my service there for every year of the war, from 1940 to 1945.

My six brothers, on the other hand, all landed in the armed forces. Jim went into the army, became a hero, and finished as a lieutenant. My mother went to Washington, D.C. to see him awarded the Purple Heart. Vincent was a Seabee and spent a good portion of his service time on the island of Guam. Francis was a career man in the navy and a specialist in mine warfare. Paul served in the army during the World War, and continued on later into Korea, as did Alfred in the navy. Charlie joined the National Guard unit in Massachusetts. After the war, he continued in the National Guard, finally retiring after twenty-two years with the rank of staff sergeant. Richard, the youngest of our family, was not old enough to be subject to the World War II draft, but did serve several years later in the Army Reserves in Massachusetts.

It wasn't very easy for us on the home front taking in the pictures and stories about what was happening overseas. We did our share of anxious waiting and praying. God was good to us: with all that McCarthy courage on the front line, not one was lost. Everybody came home safe and sound to enjoy many more years of life.

I spent my war years building ships. The work was physically demanding; most of the time I was out in the open air which was severely cold in winter and hot and humid in summer. After the decks were added, working inside created other difficulties. The air was thick with the smoke from the welding torches, and the noise from the chipping hammers was deafening. I'm sure that my hearing problems later owe something to these years. Towards the end of the war, I moved to the shipyard in Hingham where we constructed the LST's that landed the boys on the beaches of Normandy. We were able to put out one of these ships a week. Many of my good friends were in the D-Day invasion at Normandy. I liked to think I was helping them out.

Near the end of the war, I was also called up by the draft board. I took my physical examination at Fort Devens, Massachusetts, and was rejected because of the perforated eardrums I had left over from my bout with scarlet fever as a child. I was classified A-4F, which meant I was unfit to serve in the armed forces. Although I was happy that I would not have to kill another human being, or get shot up myself, I was disappointed, too. Working in the shipyard was a way of contributing to the war effort, but it was nothing compared to facing the enemy on the frontlines. Furthermore, A-4F was not a popular term in those days. Any healthy looking, able-bodied man not in uniform was considered a draft dodger and a coward. The papers were full of stories about men who had even injured themselves to be classified A-4F so they wouldn't have to fight. On top of that, whenever I went out with a girl, I had to face the angry eyes of teenagers who thought that I was stealing their older brother's girlfriend while he was fighting for his country overseas. We all knew the song the Andrew Sisters were singing, "Don't sit under the apple tree with anyone else but me . . ."

The truth of the matter was that I wasn't interested in any girl, nor was I looking to get involved with anyone. I went out periodically because I liked to be with someone, dance, and have a good time. I did weaken once, though, and had a tough time trying to break up the relationship later. This girl took a liking to me and she was pretty serious. I liked her, but not to the same degree. When I started to lose interest, she kept coming after me and even made excuses to visit my house. Once, I found her at home setting my mother's hair! She tried everything to get me interested again, but I just wasn't biting. I didn't want to get close to anyone in a romantic way. I knew what I had in my heart, and marriage wasn't it.

My rejection from military service raised another specter in my brain. If I was unfit to serve my country in the armed forces, what about the priesthood? Would I be rejected from serving my God? The dream that I had nourished secretly in my heart through the difficult years after my father's departure seemed to be threatened yet again, this time by my health. If my country wouldn't take me, would my Church? I could feel despair clutching at my heart. What was I going to do?

One day, as I was going by a church, I popped inside and went over to the statue of the Blessed Virgin Mary. I told her my story: I had been rejected from serving in the armed forces. Would this also prevent me from serving God? I made a "deal" with the Blessed Virgin. As I knelt at the foot of her statue, I promised that I would say the rosary every day of my life if I would somehow be accepted into the priesthood. As I write this story now, in the Jubilee Year of Our Lord, with forty-eight years of priesthood under my belt, I can tell you that the Blessed Mother kept her promise to me and, with rare exceptions, I have kept my promise to her.

My best friend during these years was Chester Balinski. We grew up together in South Boston. I remember Chester in our younger days, tall and blonde, with the physique of an athlete. He was also a great pool shark whom nobody could beat. At one point, I helped him get a job at the shipyard, but he later found a position at Gillette's razor factory where he worked most of his life.[4]

---

[4] Chet passed away in December 2001.

One summer, Chester and I managed to start a criminal record together. We used to go, from time to time, to Carson Beach, the popular swimming beach for the "lower enders" of South Boston. It stretches in a long inlet from where the John F. Kennedy Library now stands to the famous "L" Street bathhouse built by the WPA during the Great Depression. There was a law then requiring men to wear tops to their bathing suits. One day, Chester and I, shirtless, were standing on the topside of the beach near the sidewalk when all of a sudden two policemen walked up to us and placed us under arrest for appearing naked from the waist up. They took us to a waiting "paddy wagon," as we called them in those days, and along with a number of other men caught for the same "crime," we were taken to the police station and booked. My mother had to come bail me out. I was embarrassed, to say the least. I can laugh about this exploit now, but at the time it wasn't very funny. By necessity, the story has stayed with me. When I fill out registration forms and come to the place where it says, "Have you ever been arrested for a crime?" I have a difficult time explaining that I was arrested for not wearing a top to my bathing suit one hot day in August in my late teens.

Another anecdote from this period still gives me a small burst of pride. One Sunday night, I went to hear the famous Sammy Kaye Orchestra at Loew's Theater in downtown Boston. The marquee read, "Swing and Sway with Sammy Kaye." If you know your big band history at all then you know that Sammy Kaye was one of the biggest. At a certain point in the show, Sammy Kaye asked for volunteers to compete in a "lead the band" contest. I immediately put up my hand. Even though I was sitting way up high in the theater, Sammy Kaye picked me to join the contest. I speedily worked my way down to the stage. I don't remember the song the band was playing while I was "directing," but when it was over I was chosen the best. And that was not the end of the story. All the winners were supposed to appear for a final contest the last night of the orchestra's engagement, after which, Sammy Kaye himself would select the final winner. Since the final competition was a weeknight and I was working nights during this period, I had to take time off from work so that I could compete. I decided to go for it. When my turn came, I led the band in the song *Put on Your Old Gray Bonnet*. As the band started to play, I got into the "swing" of things. When I heard some of my friends cheering me on from the back of the theatre I really got into the mood and responded by waving my baton like I really knew what I was doing.

I never imagined I would actually win this contest. I didn't think of myself as the winner sort. Well, lo and behold, I won! This was a wonderful, new feeling – to have accomplished something important in people's eyes. I had never succeeded at anything before. The guys from work were suitably impressed when they picked me up the next night. They were really proud of me.

It would have been easy to lose my way with all that was happening in my life. I was a busy young man with a lot of responsibilities. I liked having a good time, too. It wouldn't have been hard for me to follow the path that all my friends were on: find a nice girl, get married, and settle down. Fortunately, my Heavenly Father was watching over me. Sometime during the last year of the war, I had an unusual experience that served to solidify my vocation and keep me on track. I never mentioned this event to anyone. I have kept it locked away in my heart all these years. But now that I am tracing the path I followed into the priesthood, it seems the right moment to tell the tale.

One Saturday night, I was dancing with a beautiful girl. Actually, all I can remember about her was that she was tall and wore a red dress that made her stand out amidst all those dancing couples. She was a good dancer and I was enjoying myself, when all of a sudden I heard a voice say, "Tom, I don't want you to waste your time dancing with this lovely young lady. I want you to follow me. I have some great things I want you to do for me." I don't remember seeing any face or image. I just heard this voice telling me to follow Him.

I was amazed. I could not believe what I was hearing. I thought that people got messages from heaven in a church or when they are meditating on the Lord. I thought you had to be a special kind of person. Here I was, just a shipyard employee from Southie, dancing with a girl in the middle of a crowded floor. It was as if someone had pointed at me and then beckoned me away with his finger.

The desire to be a priest moved from the backburner to the front of my thoughts. It was all I could think about. And the more I longed to be a priest, the more unhappy I was at work and discontented with a life that didn't seem to be going anywhere. I had been there for my family after my father left. I had been there for my country during the war. Now that the war was winding down, the future began to open up for me again. I knew that my brothers would be home soon and that they could look after themselves and Mom. It was my turn now.

Looking back on these years, I realize now that God was really answering my prayer to become a priest. He was preparing me with his own kind of seminary training: the real world. I got in touch with the life of the ordinary working person who has to go out and give it a full eight-hour effort five days a week, if not more. I could draw from this experience later to understand and comfort the people God sent me. Having grown up with an abusive alcoholic, in a "dysfunctional family," as they say nowadays, I was better able to help people later in these same difficulties. By having to wait for the realization of my dream, I learned the virtue of patience and the need to have faith even in the most impossible situations. Despite what I might have thought then, these years were not a waste of time. I was being prepared for my role as priest, teacher, pastor, and hospital chaplain, not to mention my work in Marriage Encounter, Retrouvaille, and Beginnings Experience. Every brick was being carefully laid in the foundation of my priestly life.

During my early days at the shipyard, I had promised myself and God that when the war was over I would immediately go into the seminary – anyplace that would accept me – no matter what. I had tried to get into the Boston Archdiocese, but the priest I talked with told me that without attending Boston College High School, I could forget it. He wasn't very positive about my vocation. He didn't even encourage me to check out other possibilities, like religious orders or other dioceses. I was surprised at that – but, since I wasn't familiar with the world of religious communities, I just went back to my everyday life thinking that becoming a priest was probably a hopeless idea.

Still, the hopeless idea did not go away.

And then, once again, my violin lesson was the scene of my unfolding vocation story. One day on my way in for a lesson, I bumped into Father John Burke who had recently been ordained a priest in the Clerics of St. Viator. He had come home to Boston to say his first Mass and was just popping in to Katherine Sullivan's to say hello. John had also been one of Katherine's violin students and we had known each other a long time. I told him about my dilemma and asked him to intercede for me with the Viatorian provincial. He said he would. We were in the month of August 1945. The war had just been declared over. I was twenty-five years old. It was now or never.

I didn't expect anything to happen right away, but a few weeks later I came home one Friday night to find a letter waiting for me from Father Richard French, the Viatorian provincial. He said simply that I was accepted to the Clerics of St. Viator and I could come now and begin college at Loyola University in Chicago in September, or else wait until next June. Then and there, with the letter in my hand, I decided to leave immediately. I really did not know too much about Chicago. I certainly didn't know anything about the Viatorians. The only thing I knew was that they wanted me to come and be part of their community. They were going to let me become a priest.

I knew what I wanted to do, but I had to make sure everything would be okay for Mom. After all, this wasn't a decision that affected me alone; for her it meant the loss of a son and a salary. She listened quietly and then said, with characteristic common sense, "If you died we would have to get along without you." Her practicality didn't hide, however, her happiness and pride for what I was about to embark upon.

The next day, Saturday, I went out and bought a black suit and a one-way ticket to Chicago.

Receiving that letter from Father French was one of the happiest moments of my life. I could not have known all the implications of my choice, nor could I have imagined the difficulties that lay ahead. I just knew I was on the way to my goal. I was going to realize my dream. I have never forgotten what Father French did for me, accepting me "sight unseen" as he did. He didn't question me about money or education. He didn't even have me go through the standard psychological testing program that most communities have today. He just said, "Come!"

I didn't need to be told twice.

A New Family

When I left for Chicago, I was really plunging ahead in faith. I knew nothing of the religious congregation to which I was destined. Even though the Clerics of St. Viator had a mission in Marlboro, Massachusetts, teaching high school in the French speaking community, I had never heard of them. It didn't matter. I had only one thing on my mind: to be a priest. I didn't care where or with whom. The Clerics of St. Viator had said they would take me. That was all I needed to know.

Looking back now on my life, on my journey of faith, it is clear to me that nothing happened by accident. My Heavenly Father was looking out for me and it was His plan that I enter the Clerics of St. Viator. The charism of the Viatorians turned out to be my charism exactly. I can sum it up in three words: service, witness, and relationship. Over the years, I have discovered that I have the personality of a "helper." I'm no leader. My happiest moments are spent in service to someone who needs assistance. I have also learned that, despite the wounds of my father's abandonment, or maybe because of them, the most important thing for me is relationship. I am happiest when I am part of a family. Learning to strengthen the intimacy between couples as a Marriage Encounter priest has been one of my life's greatest joys. And finally, thanks to little Audrey Santo and the bleeding host, the ordinary witness I give as a priest to the Real Presence of Christ in the Eucharist has become a unique apostolate.

All of this, the essence of my life, as it were, was there to discover in the history and spirituality of the Clerics of St. Viator, though it took me a lifetime. In the beginning it was as simple as this: the Viatorians accepted me and I went.

The Viatorians

Most Americans have probably never heard of the Clerics of St. Viator. I have grown accustomed to meeting blank stares when I give the name of my congregation; on the other hand, there have been occasions when I have been pleasantly surprised to discover that the Viatorian presence was known and appreciated. Our symbol expresses the spirit of our ministry: "Sinite Parvulos Venire Ad Me" ("Let the little children come to me." Mt 19:14).

The Clerics of St. Viator date their origins from the inspiration of Father Louis-Joseph Marie Querbes (pronounced, "Curbs") about the year 1830.[5] Recognizing the Church's need for help in post-revolutionary France, Father Querbes founded the Clerics of St. Viator, choosing as patron a Lyonese saint of the fourth century celebrated for

---

[5] This short history of the Clerics of St. Viator is taken from three sources: Viatorian Father George J. Auger's free and abridged translation of the biography *Louis Querbes* by Léo Bonneville, C.S.V., available on request from the Clerics of St. Viator; the pamphlet, *The Mary-Hearted Catechist*, prepared by the Louis Querbes Commission of Our Lady of Arlington, Arlington Heights, Illinois, 1955; and the article *Clerics of Saint Viator* in the Catholic Encyclopedia, 1913 edition.

his fidelity to the service of the Church, particularly in catechesis. Father Querbes also found in St. Viator's story something he hoped would mark his clerics: personal holiness and fraternal love. In fact, St. Viator's story is really the story of two men. You can't speak about one without reference to the other.

In Latin the name Viator means "wayfarer" or "traveler." The word was used in Roman law to describe a minor court official who summoned people to appear before the magistrate. This may have been St. Viator's occupation before he entered the service of the Church, or it may refer to his family of origin. We don't know if Viator was a convert to the Faith or not; in any case, tradition tells us that he served as a lector in the Diocese of Lyon. In those days, this position was accorded much more responsibility and respect than in our own time. Lectors had the specific task of educating Catholic youth and catechumens in the beliefs of the Church. In order to do this, they attended a special school where they received a literary and religious education. The bishop conferred their office upon them in an official liturgical rite that included a special consecratory prayer, reception of the book of the Scriptures, and a commission to read the Scriptures during the liturgy. St. Viator was a very able and energetic lector in his diocese. Ancient hagiographers (people who write the histories of the saints) describe Viator as "a most holy youth who, on account of his eminent virtues, was much beloved by his bishop."

The bishop in question was St. Just, a man of recognized holiness who had risen to the episcopate of Lyon sometime after 343 A.D. Bishop Just was evidently a very sensitive man who took his responsibilities as bishop very seriously; so seriously, in fact, that he was unable to live with what he considered a terrible error on his part. One day, a madman in a violent rage ran through the market swinging a sword right and left, wounding and killing some of the townspeople. He then ran into the church and asked for asylum. St. Just wanted to protect the man, but the angry townspeople cleverly convinced him that the man would receive a fair trial if he were released to them. St. Just gave in to their demands. No sooner was the poor unfortunate outside the safe confines of the church than he was grasped from the hands of the magistrates and put to death by the vengeful mob. The good bishop felt responsible for the man's death. He believed that he had failed as a pastor and that this error would forever cripple his authority as bishop, making him unfit to serve his people. He wanted to turn his see over to more capable hands and devote the rest of his life to prayer and penance.

Knowing that his people would not willingly let him go, St. Just confided to his friend Viator his intention to become a hermit and then left secretly for Egypt. Viator wasn't long to catch up with him. Together, the two friends found their way to the Libyan Desert where they joined a strict monastic community and devoted their lives to fasting, prayer, and silence. Within their community, they remained anonymous. One day, however, a pilgrim from Lyon recognized Just and Viator and begged them to return with him. They refused. The pilgrim subsequently informed the diocese of their whereabouts and a certain Antiochus was sent to retrieve them. His efforts also failed. Bishop Just died soon after, probably of old age. As always, Viator was not long to follow. It seems that grief at the loss of his friend and the rigors of desert life proved too much for him.

What the Lyonese could not accomplish by the living consent of Just and Viator, they were able to achieve after their deaths. The two bodies were returned to Lyon and given the same veneration accorded to martyrs (at this time, in fact, monastic life was understood to be "white martyrdom," a martyrdom without blood.) Something about the story of Just and Viator captivated the Lyonese. The memory of the two friends soon overshadowed that of their more famous predecessors in Lyon so that, by the fifth century, four feast days annually celebrated their lives. In 1287, their relics were found to be in the same tomb along with documents attesting to their holy lives. Unfortunately, these relics went on to suffer the painful history of Catholicism in France. Threatened first by the Calvinists in 1562, and then again by anti-Catholic mobs during the revolution, they rest today in the Church of St. Just in Lyon, a poignant reminder of the damage done by wars over religion.

Louis Querbes knew all about this kind of damage. He was born on August 21, 1793, right in the middle of the French Revolution as his native city of Lyon lay under siege. His father had him baptized immediately because of the danger; in fact, the very next day a bomb obliterated the family home. Even after the shelling stopped, the times were perilous for faithful Catholics.

Louis learned his faith and prayers at his mother's knee. At a relatively early age he made a personal consecration of himself to God by a vow of perpetual chastity. He was educated in his parish of St. Nizier in Lyon. The parish church stood on the site of the ancient Church of the Holy Apostles where St. Just had presided as bishop and St. Viator had served as lector.

Louis eventually entered St. Irenaeus, the major seminary of the Archdiocese of Lyon, where he excelled in his studies. God was certainly providing for the reconstruction of Catholic France: On June 23, 1815, the day of Louis's sub-diaconate ordination, he stood with a class that included St. John Vianney, the future Curé of Ars, John Claude Colin, founder of the Marist Fathers, and Marcellin Champagnat, founder of the Marist Brothers.

After his priestly ordination in 1816, Louis returned to his home parish where he served as associate pastor and teacher in the school. In 1822, he was appointed pastor of the Church of St. Bonnet in Vourles, a nearby village. Despite offers of more glamorous positions in the hierarchy, Louis retained his humble role in Vourles for the rest of his life.

Early on in his career, Father Querbes saw the need for a society of lay catechists who could assist pastors in the work of the Church and the teaching of youth. The situation was desperate. France had been ravaged by the French Revolution and the Reign of Terror. Monasteries, convents, and churches had been ransacked and religious and priests thrown into prison, exiled, or sentenced to the guillotine. Strong public sentiment against the Church continued throughout the early 19th century. In many places it seemed that the Church was paralyzed. Throughout the country, a gap existed where the Church had once provided for education and culture.

As early as 1829, Father Querbes was running a school for the education and formation of laymen. His idea to use laymen, however, was about a hundred and fifty years ahead of its time. The bishop of Lyon did not share his enthusiasm and asked that the men who worked with him be priests or brothers. Hence, in 1835, Father Querbes's devoted little band was formed into the Clerics of St. Viator. In 1838, they received the approval of Pope Gregory XVI. A touching part of the Viatorian story is the hospitality and guidance offered to Father Querbes by the Roman Jesuits during his long stay in Rome. Father Querbes held the Jesuit order in great esteem.

Over the next twenty-six years, Father Louis Querbes saw the rapid growth of his congregation. Besides parochial schools, the Viatorians branched out into boarding colleges, education of the deaf, and schools of agriculture. They also had a publishing house from which they sent out schoolbooks and educational magazines. In their publications, the Clerics of St. Viator upheld the need for co-operation between parent, pastor, and teacher in the education of youth.

In 1847, in response to an appeal from Bishop Bourget of Montreal, Father Querbes sent teachers to serve at a small college in Joliette, Canada. Soon after, the Clerics of St. Viator opened a novitiate in the same city. While the Clerics flourished in Canada, an attempt at a foundation in St. Louis in 1842 failed to take root. The first successful foundations in the United States came once again in response to the need of French-Canadian settlers who had migrated to the Bourbonnais Grove, Illinois area. From there, the Clerics spread out to Kankakee, St. George, Aurora, and Chicago. Later, they went into New York and as far as the state of Oregon. While in France and Canada the order had been known as the Clerics of Saint Viator; the term "Viatorians" was coined in the United States.

In 1882, the Viatorian establishments of the Midwestern United States became independent of the Canadian province. Father Cyrille Fournier was the first superior of the newly created province. He immediately opened a novitiate in Bourbonnais, though this plus the provincial administrative headquarters were moved to Chicago in 1888. Father

Fournier served as head of the American Viatorians for twenty-five years and left the order with a well-trained force of teachers. The most important institution of the Viatorians in the United States was St. Viator College in Bourbonnais, which included Bishop Fulton J. Sheen among its alumni.[6]

Taking the Shape of a Viatorian

By the Providence of God, I had landed into this prodigious congregation. It remained to be seen if I would make it to the finish line. I wasn't the first South Bostonian that the Viatorians had welcomed. My friend Father John Burke grew up in Southie. He had lived on the third floor of the tenement apartment building on the corner of "L" and Eighth Streets, over the famous "L" Street Tavern. Father Pat Flaherty, C.S.V., also came from South Boston. He died on July 19, 1943, while serving in the army. He is honored in Southie with a street-sign plaque in the "D" Street project located in the Lower End.

So, now it was my turn. At the age of twenty-five, I was what I liked to describe as a "delayed" vocation. Already a fully formed adult with specific habits of thinking and acting, my first challenge was to leave behind me my South Boston ways and take on the manner and bearing of a man of God. The setting for this was to be the provincial house in Chicago. Normally, Viatorian religious went to Ambrose College in Davenport, Iowa, but Brother Leo Prince, the procurator at our provincial house, needed someone who could drive him around to do the shopping. I was it. This wouldn't be the first time my age and experience contributed to my assignment.

---

[6] The college was closed in 1938.

The provincial house actually consisted of four large homes on the Lake Michigan side of North Sheridan Road and Granville Street, just a few blocks south of Loyola University, North Shore Campus. I had a fifteen-minute walk everyday to school, which also took me past the former Mundelein College for girls (now part of the Loyola complex).

Coming from the city streets of South Boston, I heartily appreciated living on beautiful Lake Michigan with its dramatic change of seasons. Summers were warm but pleasant and the swimming beach on Granville boasted quite a crowd. Winter wore a very different face. On many occasions, I saw icicles hanging on the power lines around the lake, formed by the bitter cold and the water of the leaping waves beneath. At certain times of the year, weather conditions could change rapidly. I can remember one day, while I was waiting for the bus to go downtown, the temperature dropped from a nice seventy degrees to a rather unpleasant forty degrees. Natives of the area are fond of saying, "If you don't like the weather, wait a minute. It'll change."

The greatest hurdle before me was my lack of education. I simply was not ready for college. I should have gone first to a preparatory school of some kind; instead, my provincial threw me into the lions' den at Loyola University. It was a tough year. I didn't know how to study. I would read the same stuff over and over again, but it wouldn't stick. I studied so hard for my history courses that I strained my eyes and had to get glasses. My English grammar was so bad that I had to take a special course for "dummies" to help me prepare for English 101. My English professor couldn't understand how I got into college. To tell you the truth, I couldn't understand it either.

No one helped me and, sad to say, I never asked for any help. The self-sufficiency I had learned as the premature father of a family of eight made it nearly impossible for me to ask for assistance. I was used to keeping quiet and solving problems on my own. Now, face to face with this academic challenge, I followed the same practice. I tried to lie low and fight my way through it alone. That was stupid of me. If there is one thing I'd like to pass on to all those who read this book, it's this: Don't be afraid to ask for help!

I took Latin at night school on the downtown campus and passed only because the teacher took pity on me. I really did not know what I was doing. I used a "pony," an English translation of the Latin, to help me translate the assigned texts and rode on my pony whenever I was called upon to recite. I knew that I couldn't pass the final exam, but the Latin teacher passed me anyway. Evidently, his daughter had married a Catholic priest – something he did not like at all – and so he was inclined to pass me because, as he said, "You may not be a Latin scholar, but at least you are living your vows of celibacy." In the end, I had four years of Latin without ever really learning the language.

Giving credit where credit is due, I have to say that the only reason I survived my first year as a religious and a student was due to the intervention of the Blessed Virgin. She took me by the hand and cleared the way before me. She remembered the pact we had made. I learned to just keep putting my trust in her.

Novitiate

After my first year of college, I was sent to Bourbonnais, Illinois, to do my novitiate year, from August 18, 1946, to August 19, 1947 – one year and a day.

Nowadays, there's more emphasis on the spiritual nature of the novitiate year. It's meant to be a time of deepening in the interior life, a time to listen to the Holy Spirit to discern the direction in which God is calling. In my day, the character of novitiate year was a little more rugged, more like "boot camp" for religious. You can't be a fulltime soldier if you don't do boot camp. You couldn't be a religious without doing novitiate. But at least boot camp was only for three months. We had one full year in novitiate! I know that a good number of other communities required two years of novitiate. One year was quite enough for me.

Maybe the dramatic nature of my novitiate year had something to do with the surroundings. Bourbonnais was the first place in the United States where the Viatorians really took root. They had come to repair damage done by a renegade priest named Father Charles Chiniquy. As a young religious, I was fascinated by this story. I would like to take a moment to share it with you, especially since it sheds some light on what brought the Viatorians to the United States.

Charles Chiniquy was born in 1809 in Kamouraska, Quebec. After the death of his parents, his uncle adopted him, but eventually cut him off financially for his immoral conduct. For some reason, Charles decided to become a priest. Early on in the seminary he established a reputation for controversy. He did not accept teachings that were not specifically spelled out in the Bible. He had doubts about confession, the Immaculate Conception, the Assumption, and Church authority. He bumped heads with his superiors on several occasions; nevertheless, he succeeded in being ordained at the age of 42. He was a gifted orator, and thanks to the publication of his book *The Manual of Temperance*, he had the reputation, if not the being, of a holy man. He buffered his position by showing off a gold crucifix he had received from the Pope through his bishop.

Father Chiniquy was assigned the pastorate of Maternity Church of the Blessed Virgin Mary in Bourbonnais; however, upon his arrival, he discovered that the church already had a pastor. Undaunted, he struck out on his own to find a congregation and landed at St. Anne's Church in a town called Beaver Creek about twelve miles south of Kankakee, Illinois. Without the bishop's appointment, he installed himself there as pastor. At that time, St. Anne's had about a hundred parishioners, but Father Chiniquy had big plans. He advertised in Canada that with only $200.00 you could become rich in Illinois. Despite the bishop of Chicago's public refutation of Chiniquy's claims, hundreds of fortune hunters responded to the advertisement and streamed into the area from Canada.

Then, in September 1853, Maternity Church in Bourbonnais mysteriously went down in flames. Suspicion arose about Chiniquy's involvement in the blaze and he was eventually brought to court. Even with the eloquent defense of a young Illinois lawyer named Abraham Lincoln, Chiniquy's trial ended in a hung jury. Doubts continued to linger about Chiniquy's involvement in the fire. The bishop had had enough. On August 19, 1856, he suspended Chiniquy, stripping him of the right to function as a Catholic priest. Later, the vicar general of the Chicago Diocese formally excommunicated Chiniquy and forced him to give up the pastorate of St. Anne's Church in Beaver Creek. Unrepentant, Chiniquy announced to the people that he was no longer a priest but would continue to lead his congregation, most of whom continued to follow him. He then proceeded to take over the church of St. Anne, which legally belonged to the Diocese of Chicago. Amazingly, a circuit court who later heard the case decided in Chiniquy's favor and he remained pastor of St. Anne's until 1896. The loss of St. Anne's to the true Catholic community meant that between 1858 and 1871 the Catholic people did not have a church building of their own.

The people of Bourbonnais had quite a year in 1865. On April 2, Lee surrendered to General Ulysses S. Grant at Appomattox. Just a few weeks later, Illinois's favorite son was assassinated and the entire nation went into mourning. Then, word came that an order of religious priests and brothers were coming from Montreal to assume the pastorate of Maternity Church and establish a boys' school and college. In fact, the Viatorians came like medicine into this broken and hurting community. Thanks to Chiniquy's schemes, the area was largely French-speaking. The Canadian Viatorians were able to minister to the people and undo some of the damage done by Chiniquy. This was the beginning of Viatorian ministry in the United States of America.

Our novitiate was located across the street from Mount Olivet College, a Nazarene school that had once been run by the Viatorians under the name of St. Viator College. The building was a former dormitory for the college. Long and uncomfortable, it was hot in summer and freezing in winter. I often had the job of firing the boiler by shoveling coal into the furnace.

We received the habit at the beginning of our novitiate. It consisted of a long black, button down robe that was fitted around the waist with a three knotted cord. The three knots symbolized the three vows of poverty, chastity, and obedience. At the end of our novitiate year, we took temporary vows of three years. After this period, if we wished to continue, and if the community accepted us, we were allowed to renew our vows for another three years. At the completion of these six years in temporary vows, and subject to a community vote, we were allowed to take our final or perpetual vows.

We rose every day at 5:30 A.M. when the "regulator" would wake us up with the ringing of a large bell. He would knock on our door and sing out at the top of his lungs, "Benedicamus Domino" Then, we would have to let him know that we heard him by answering, "Deo Gratias!" Meditation began at 6:00 A.M. A brother was assigned to read the minutes of meditation from a book used by the Jesuits. There were three points of meditation. As you can imagine, at this early hour of the morning it was none too easy to stay awake. The novice master, Father Roger Drolet, a lovely person but a strict disciplinarian, would gently tap the shoulder of a novice who was starting to nod. The guilty party was then obliged to slide off the bench and kneel on the floor. It was a wooden floor and, I can tell you from personal experience, pretty hard.

In the novitiate, we had what was known as "accusation day." You had to kneel before the novice master and confess any transgressions of which you were guilty. A novice would confess things like, "I broke a plate while washing dishes" or "I called one of the other novices a lazy and uncooperative person because he is not pulling his weight around here and I am sick and tired of his non-conforming attitude." The novice master would then give a few words of spiritual advice and, for our penance, ask us to kiss the floor. We all laugh about this now. I don't know if we would do it today. At that time, I didn't care. I just wanted to get through with the novitiate year and continue my college studies so that I could get into the seminary and get ordained. One-track mind!

Overall, novitiate was a time of discernment, an opportunity to think about making the religious life our whole life. Actually, the discernment went both ways: we looked at the Viatorians, and they looked at us. Being under the microscope, as it were, lent a bit of drama to our life as novices.

In a certain way, novitiate was one of the greatest times of my life. I was able to do all the things that I really wanted to do: attend Mass every day, spend time meditating on spiritual books, and enjoy the company of my brothers. There were about twenty of us in the novitiate. Living in a rural community had some advantages. On days off, we were allowed to go out and play baseball in the local field. I would leave the game a little earlier than the others to fire up the boiler so that we could have some hot water for our showers.

During this year, I had no contact with my family. We were not allowed any home visits, nor did my family come to see me. My mother was too busy with the family, and my brothers were slowly making the adjustment to civilian life again after the war. They were all too occupied to worry about me. Father John Burke, the man who had introduced me to the Viatorians, never came down to visit me or see how I was getting along. I was more than a bit lonely on visiting days when I saw the other guys with their families around. I realized that my own brothers and I had never had the chance to get really close. When they were young, I was busy supporting the family. Then the war came and they were called up for military service. When they got back, I left for the seminary. I never felt any bitterness towards my family for not visiting me. I understood.

Just as we were getting into the swing of it in Bourbonnais, our time there came to an end. On Thanksgiving Day, the Clerics of St. Viator sold the novitiate house and all of us were transferred back to North Sheridan Road and Granville Street in Chicago. We had to change our daily routine from the rural style of agricultural Bourbonnais to the suburban style of Chicago. We couldn't go out to the field and play baseball, for one thing. Instead, for exercise we had to walk down busy Sheridan Road to one of the nearby churches, St. Gertrude's, or the university chapel at Loyola. Father Drolet built a high wall so that we novices would not be distracted by all those good-looking girls walking around in their bikinis on Granville beach.

I had received my habit on August 18, 1946, in Bourbonnais. One year later, on the Feast of the Assumption of the Blessed Virgin Mary, I made my temporary vows. It was only fitting that I make my vows on this great feast of Our Lady since I had committed my vocation to her. She has seen me through the good times and the bad times. Without her support, I don't think that I would ever have become a priest. All the extraordinary things that have happened to me have been through her intercession. She has been my guardian, my constant friend and close companion.

The usual course for a religious just completing the novitiate was to resume his college education. Father French asked me to stay on at the provincial house and continue into my second year of studies at Loyola University. The main reason for keeping me in Chicago was Brother Prince's ongoing need for a driver. I felt bad about this turn of events because all my confreres – with whom I had just spent one intense year – returned to St. Ambrose College in Davenport, Iowa, to complete their college studies. I felt somewhat left behind.

Nevertheless, back I went to Loyola. It is still a wonder to me that I finished my degree, considering the kind of academic preparation I didn't have. Just to give you an idea of how close I came to missing the boat: During my last year at Loyola, the faculty issued a directive that every student would have to take an exam in their major field in order to graduate. I was not up to that and I knew it. Fortunately, the launching date for the new edict was just after I would finish. I wouldn't have to take the test. Need I say how much I was relieved? Once again, the Blessed Virgin had interceded for me.

With the help of summer school courses at De Paul University in Chicago, I managed to meet the requirements of Loyola University for a Ph.B. degree in philosophy with a psychology minor. I received my degree in June 1949. I couldn't get a Bachelor of Arts degree because I needed two foreign languages – not likely considering I had just scraped by in Latin thanks to the generosity of my Latin professor.

Usually, after graduation, the community sends a brother out to teach for a year or two. My provincial, Father French, waived this practice in my case in consideration of my age. I think that he liked me, too – and this, coupled with the fact that he needed priests at that time, moved him to send me directly on to the seminary at the Catholic University of America in Washington, D.C. I was happy about that! I was twenty-nine years old and setting out for the capital!

From Dream to Reality

In those days, the fifties and sixties, the Viatorians had a house of studies in Washington, D.C., called the Theologate. When we Viatorians talk about being in the "seminary," we don't mean it in the way a diocesan priest does. The Theologate was really a religious house for our seminarians and some of our priests who taught at Catholic University. It was located on Quincy Street next to the Franciscan monastery famous for its replica of the catacombs. The house of studies for the Divine Word community was right across the street, while that of the Fathers of Mercy was just down the road a bit.

The Theologate had the size and facilities of a grand home. It was two stories high with a basement. While the ordained priests all had private rooms, we seminarians had to live together, usually about four to a room. We got to know the ins and outs of each other pretty well because of these circumstances.

We started the day with morning prayers, followed by a half-hour of meditation before Mass. The "admonitor," as we called him, set up the schedule week by week. We all took turns serving Mass, being the lector, and making breakfast afterwards. We all chipped in and did what we were able to do best. I was the chief toaster. For lunches and dinners during the week we had a great cook, Marie, who had once worked for the Kennedys. I was particularly fond of her "pop ups," but she would never give us the recipe. We all took turns driving her back home after meals. On Saturday and Sunday we did our own cooking. I was such a bad cook that my brothers would only let me make the salad. I was good at salad.

Since we were not priests we did not say the Office. We did have afternoon prayers before supper which consisted of what was called the "legend": readings from Scripture, the Imitation of Christ, a book written by Alphonse Rodriguez, or the Catechism of the Council of Trent, followed by fifteen minutes of quiet time and the rosary. Reading assignments were posted weekly on the bulletin board.

We had about a half-hour walk every day to the School of Theology at Catholic University of America. If we were lucky, we might get a ride with one of our priests teaching there. Our rector, Father John Stafford, was head of the Department of Psychology. Fathers Bernard Mulvaney, Dumas McCleary, Frank Powers, and Joe O'Brien also lived in our house and taught at the University.

While no one person had a great influence on me in the seminary, I do remember being affected by the presence of so many religious communities with their many different kinds of garb. The Dominicans stand out in my mind with their wide black belt from which hung a pair of rosary beads. I was also impressed by the habits of the Fathers of Mercy, the Brown Franciscans, the Black Franciscans, the Carmelites, the Sulpicians, as well as many others worn by the seminarians who attended the same theology classes. This was a great experience for me of the many different charisms of a Universal Church.

In those days we took poverty very seriously. We had no money in our pockets, and if we needed anything we had to ask our superior for it. His decision was final. In one instance, this fact had a somewhat comic result. On Wednesday afternoons one of the barbers in town used to come up to the Sulpician house of studies, the "Sulp house," as we called it, to cut hair. He used to charge the seminarians a cut rate, twenty-five cents, I believe. We Viatorians were welcomed to take advantage of this offer as well. One of the brothers asked Father Frederick Wenthe, the superior at the time, for twenty-five cents and a five-cent tip in order to get a hair cut. Father Wenthe looked the brother over and said to him, "You don't need a hair cut." The Good Brother respected his superior's wishes. He also decided never to ask him again for money for a haircut. Months went by – and even a year. In those days, we seminarians were not allowed to wear our hair long. Here was the Good Brother with hair down to his shoulders. I don't know what happened later between him and Father Wenthe, but the Good Brother eventually resigned from the community.

We seminarians usually ate separately from the ordained priests. The scene was what you would expect from a bunch of students, even garbed in long, black cassocks. There were stories about skipping class and hanging around at the "dug out," the place where you could buy snacks and whatnot. No class was more notorious for absences than Father Weisengoff's Scripture course. Even though there were about a hundred students registered for the course, only thirty or forty ever showed up. I have to say that I tried to attend all his classes, even though we did not learn very much Scripture. Father Weisengoff wasn't very easy to study under. On one occasion, he announced a test and told us that we could bring whatever texts we wished to the exam. A friend of mine brought in two armfuls of books, but I don't think he ever got to open one of them since the question was given in Latin. Can't win for trying.

One of our favorite stories was about Father John Beatty meeting Father Connell, O.P., at the pool. Father Connell was a highly respected, dogma professor. He looked quite imposing in his long white Dominican robe, with the wide black belt and the fifteen-decade rosary hanging at his side. Well, in those days men used to swim without any swimsuit. One day at poolside, Father Beatty met Father Connell in his birthday suit and commented, "Pardon me, Father, I didn't recognize you without your religious garb." (NB: You are all supposed to laugh.)

Another source of great amusement was how one of our theology professors liked to have the class clap their hands whenever he told stories about himself. He was fond of reminding us that while he was studying in Rome, he had been confessor for one of the popes. We would all clap and make a big din about this. Father loved it. If he showed himself to be a bit childish, at least he was consistent. He treated us like grade schoolers. He would put all the handouts on the first desks of each row and then we had to line up and go around the room and pick them up one at a time. Despite his peculiarities, he was a wonderful man and he really knew his history.

There were two programs available to us students at the time: the minor course and the major course. The major course people earned a degree, but they had to take Hebrew, and I certainly did not see the need for that in my case. I was in the minor or non-degree group. We also did four years of theology, but without getting a degree of any kind. It was, to be honest, blood, sweat and tears for us – and with nothing to show for it. Seminarians following the same courses now get a Masters of Divinity degree.

Classes were a mixed bag. Some were good, and some were caught in a time warp between traditional seminarian education and the new trends that were coming into vogue. I am talking about the years spanning 1949-1953. Latin, for example, was required in the seminary; some of the classes were even taught in Latin. One day, our theology professor was running through his lesson in Latin when all of a sudden he stopped and asked, "Do you guys understand what I am saying?" Of course, we answered a decided, "No!" He then took pity on us and changed to English. I think prestige was one of the reasons that Latin stayed on so long. The faculty felt that since Catholic University was an "Ivy League College" we had to keep up the standards.

The disinterest of some of my teachers amazed me. My spirituality professor never lifted up his head from the moment he entered the class until the end of the period. One day a student, in order to make some money, sold hot dogs during class. Somebody even had the audacity to ask for mustard. Another professor of ours who was supposed to be teaching us morality would never take up the sixth and ninth commandments. He marched through them like Grant taking Richmond.

I shouldn't be too critical of my faculty. I was nothing to write home about, either. There wasn't a single subject I didn't struggle with in some way. By God's providence and Our Lady's intercession, I made it through.

Joy and sadness marked my time in the seminary. I became very close to Deacon Ed Gallagher, one of the seminarians with the Fathers of Mercy who lived down the street from us. I used to walk down Quincy Street from our residence and wait for Ed, and then we would share the rest of the way together. On our route to school, we usually crossed a bridge over the train tracks. Sometimes, when we were in a hurry, we would skip the bridge and make a dash directly over the tracks. One particularly rainy, foggy day, Ed was rushing to Latin class and took the shortcut without looking. He was hit and killed by a train. His ordination would have taken place the following June. I think he would have made a good priest. I loved him a lot and missed him.

A big part of my seminary experience was my participation in the Catholic Students Mission Crusade (CSMC). I joined the organization when I entered the seminary and was eventually elected vice-president. In April 1952, while still a brother, I was sent to represent our chapter at the convention at Notre Dame. I was also actively engaged as the general chairman for the annual CSMC oratorical contest for which I succeeded in rounding up a number of distinguished Washington, D.C., celebrities to serve as judges.

As the vice-president of CSMC, it was my responsibility to mail out on request a free book on the priesthood. I received many inquiries from girls who wanted a similar book on communities for women in the United States, but we had nothing to send them. I conceived the idea of putting such a book together, but I was a little daunted by the idea. Me? Write a book on all the nuns in the U.S.A.? You must be crazy, I told myself, you can't pass Latin and you're dreaming of writing books! Talk about delusions of grandeur.

Somebody in heaven must have been behind this project because I received the inspiration and the courage to go see Father Magner, the treasurer of Catholic University of

America Press. I told him about my idea and, to my amazement, he was interested. He asked me to go back home and draw up a sample page for him to see; then, he would give me his answer. I did just that. When he saw what I had in mind, he was delighted and agreed to publish the book. In 1952, I finished *The Guide to the Catholic Sisterhoods in the United States*. The first edition was published that year with four more editions to follow. It was a best seller for the Catholic University of America Press.

As I approached the end of my studies, Latin became a problem for me again. I paid attention in class, but I could not pass the final exam in order to be ordained. I am amazed now to remember how scared I was over something that I would never use in all the days of my priesthood. I had to go see the Latin professor personally to find out what he was going to do about me. This was one of those occasions when God really interceded for me through someone. The professor's secretary, Molly, came to my defense. Just when things looked bleakest, she said, "Doctor, do you know that Brother McCarthy has just published a book with the Catholic University called *The Guide to the Catholic Sisterhoods in the United States?*" He said that he did not know. "How many books have you published?" queried Molly. This comment hit the mark. The professor gave in and passed me. I guess he thought that if I could get a book published by the prestigious Catholic University of America Press, then I was worthy enough to receive a passing grade so that I could be ordained. Thank God Molly was brave enough to challenge him. She saved my life and my dream to be a priest. I am ever so grateful to her. I am also grateful to the Blessed Virgin who I feel was really at work influencing that Latin professor in my favor.

A Dream Realized

1952 was a great year for me. On June 7, I received my sub-diaconate; the next day, I was ordained deacon. Usually a full year must pass after the diaconate before a man can be ordained a priest. In my case, due to the shortage of priests, this practice was waived. I became a "simplex priest" since I was ordained four months into my diaconate year. I guess I could say that the need for priests was another avenue my Heavenly Father used to move my vocation along.

I was ordained on October 1, 1952, by Bishop John McNamara at St. Gabriel Church in Washington, D.C. Students from the church school were in attendance, as well as my mother, my brother Alfred, and my violin teacher Katherine Sullivan. After the ceremony, Father John Stafford threw a fantastic dinner celebration at the Theologate. He even got some of the University's silverware to use at the party. I was honored to have present the Most Reverend Patrick McCormick, D.D., *rector magnificus* of the Catholic University of America. Outstanding in my memory of that day, however, is the joy I felt as I gave my first priestly blessing to my mother, my brother Al, and Katherine Sullivan.

Since I was not connected with a particular church, I said my first Mass the next day in our community chapel at the Theologate.

Right after ordination, I was sent out on the circuit to say Masses in the different parishes in Maryland. One thing that has stayed with me through the years is the memory of racial discrimination that I witnessed in the South. Being from the largely white region of Boston (as it then was), I had little experience with this kind of prejudice. I was astounded by the rigid separation between the races. Some of the churches I visited had two baptismal fonts, one for the whites and one for the blacks. During Mass, black parishioners sat in the back seats of the church while the white parishioners sat up front. Then, at communion time, the blacks came up to communion last. Even the confessionals were separated. I could not believe it, but there it was. This was happening in our Catholic churches in Maryland. I don't know about Washington, D.C., because I was only sent to serve churches in the nearby Maryland area.

Eventually, I was able to work my way back to my hometown of South Boston to say a first Mass at St. Augustine's Church, my mother's parish. We had a pretty large gathering, so we used the local veteran's hall for the reception afterwards. My whole family was there, as well as most of the friends and neighbors with whom I had grown up. I was the star of the day. Later, I gave the special blessing of the newly ordained to each of my family and friends. Just a few years ago I had been in this same city, working and waiting, wondering if I would ever realize my dream to be a priest. What marvels God does for us!

A letter from my sister Terry in 1999 revealed to me how my family felt about my ordination:

Father Tom,

When you decided to enter the priesthood, Mom and I were very pleased. When you left [home], I felt very bad because you had to be away so long . . . Your first Mass was the most beautiful thing in my life, watching and listening to you – my big brother with the whole Church . . . and the look on

Mom's face. Tears came down both of us
knowing you belong to us. Now when you say
Mass, it's my brother up there and I sure am
proud. Mom was the proudest, knowing you were
something special. You have a very special life.
You are warm and always [give] your heart to
everyone. You are very talented and I wish I was
a little like you.

Hearing confessions during my first year was a blessing
I can never forget. I couldn't believe the awesome power that
God had given me to act in His Name and forgive sins. I
remember hearing the anguish and sorrow in the voices of
the penitents as they confessed their sins – and then, after the
absolution, the sigh of relief. By the words that I pronounced
as a priest of God, I had the power to reconcile souls to God.
It was wonderful; it was breathtaking.

The other privilege I enjoyed greatly was baptizing
babies. My first baptism, though, will always stand out in my
mind.

I was visiting a patient in the emergency room at the
hospital when a nurse came in to ask me for help in the
delivery room. I went in and found a young mother who had
just given birth. She was crying. She knew something was
wrong with her baby and asked me to at least make sure he
was baptized. I told her I would be happy to do so and went
to find the child. I was not prepared for what I saw. For some
strange reason only known to God, the baby's head hadn't
developed. There was practically no head there at all. I was
amazed that the child had been born alive.

Baptizing a baby for the first time should be an exciting
moment for a priest. Here I was, however, without any kind
of liturgical trappings or any book from which to read. You

can imagine how nervous I felt, a rookie priest standing in the presence of nurses and staff waiting for me to perform the rite of baptism. I knew from my studies that in time of necessity all I had to do was pour the water on the child's head and say the saving words of the baptismal formula. In this case, there was no head to receive the water. I poured it on the baby's shoulder instead. I baptized him "John" because this was the name of my own little brother who had died as a child. Then I had to go into the mother and tell her the sad news. She began to sob and cry, "My baby . . . my baby." All I could do was be there for her. That seemed to be enough. After awhile she got hold of herself and thanked me.

Baby John died soon after his baptism, but I knew that from that day on I would have a little saint in heaven to pray for me and help me be a good priest.

Though I had been fortunate enough to ride the tide of circumstances to an early ordination, I still had to finish my studies. In addition to regular academic work, I also took courses over the summer. Then I had to face a French language exam. I failed the first time. Determined, I really put my mind to it and succeeded on the second attempt. Writing the thesis was another hurdle. Through the intercession of the Blessed Virgin and the providential care of my Heavenly Father, I plowed through the requirements and received the Masters Degree in Religious Education on June 9, 1953. I was, blissfully, finished with school.

Part II
A Priest of God
(1945-1996)

From Dream to Reality

"Sinite Parvulos Venire Ad Me"
(Let the Little Children Come to Me)

I had at last realized my ambition. I was a priest of God. Henceforth, it would be my honored duty to spread the Gospel and celebrate the Lord's life-giving sacraments. I was satisfied that I had reached my objective. My dream had come true. Whatever other achievements I had accomplished along the way were secondary. For a while, I just drank in the joy of being a priest. I did not care where I would be sent or what I would do. I just wanted to serve. I knew that as a Viatorian my two most likely destinations would be either teaching or parish work. My provincial decided on teaching, and that is what I did for the next twenty years.

Alleman High School – Rock Island, Illinois

My first assignment was Alleman High School in Rock Island, Illinois, in the Diocese of Peoria. I spent six wonderful years there, from 1953 to 1959. Rock Island is a river town that, at that time, boasted about 52,000 residents, a large percentage of which were of Belgian descent. Many of our students' parents worked at the Rock Island Arsenal or in the plants for the tractor companies *Harvester* and *John Deere*. Rock Island was also the home of Augustana College, a well-known Lutheran university. Though it is now a thriving metropolis, during my time there Rock Island was pretty backward. To shop, people usually went across the Mississippi to Davenport, Iowa.

I guess it's a pattern in my life to do things for which I have no preparation. While my brother Viatorians had done some teaching before entering the seminary, I had no practical experience whatsoever of the classroom. Talk about raw! Fortunately, my Heavenly Father was making the way straight before me. I was surrounded by friendly colleagues, welcoming and appreciative parents, and wonderful students.

My time at Alleman was in a way the honeymoon of my vocation. I loved teaching. I loved coming into my classroom the first day and seeing those thirty or so faces staring at me as if I were some kind of monster; then, once I started speaking, seeing them melt like ice does under the sun. These starry-eyed young people were such a blessing to me. They made it possible for me to speak about our wonderful God. I taught religion for the whole six years I was at Alleman High School and I loved doing so. After all, I became a priest because I wanted to tell everyone I met about the wonders of God, a God we cannot see but who touches our lives every day.

One lesson I tried to impart to my students was "la vida es muy corta" or "life is short." When we are young, we think we have the whole world in our hands. When we get older, we realize just how short a while we are on this earth. We must not lose any time fulfilling the plan of God in our lives. The first thing is to discern your vocation. Once you know, than you stick like glue. I could teach this with conviction because I had learned it from personal experience. No matter what the difficulties or obstacles, we must put ourselves in the hands of God and trust Him to do whatever is necessary.

One thing that helped me get off the ground at Alleman was the excellent people with whom I worked. The principal, Father John O'Connor, was not only a kind and generous leader, but a good friend, too. Every Friday morning, he would come by our faculty house and drop off a bottle of wine or some cognac. The sisters he was living with had asked him to help unload some of their wine cellar. He didn't forget us as he went about his task. Two other Viatorians I worked with, Father John "Bip" Shiels and Father John Cusack, were also good friends. They were both living at the faculty house at 1303-40th Street when I arrived. I got on particularly well with Father Shiels. He was a kind and giving person and very easy to live with.

Since many of the diocesan priests in Peoria were graduates of Viatorian schools, they knew us well and we had a great relationship with them. This good feeling was encouraged by the practice of the *Forty Hours Devotion.* When the service was over, the home parish would have a dinner for all the clergy who attended. These were wonderful, warm occasions. I was able to meet the great priests of the Rock Island deanery and experience a bond of brotherhood I had never known before my ordination or have had the good fortune to know since. Friction between religious and diocesan clergy dates back to the middle ages when religious priests and brothers were scholars and teachers while diocesan men were "lowly" parish priests who were not as well educated. Today, of course, both diocesan and religious priests are well educated, but there is still a kind of rivalry between them. Diocesan priests will always say, for example, that they were founded by St. Peter (as opposed to St. Francis, St. Dominic, etc.).

One day, I got a telephone call from Msgr. George Carton, chancellor of the Diocese of Peoria. He told me about a mother with two deaf boys who lived near the school and needed some assistance. Would I get in touch with them? Of course, I couldn't resist a request for help.

That first call to Dorothy Christensen was the beginning of a wonderful new ministry for me. Dorothy's two sons, Clark and Allen, had both graduated from Catholic schools for the deaf. They were in need of some social life. I did some checking around and found some other deaf people in the area who wanted to be included in whatever I had in mind for them. My first activity was a Mass just for the deaf. I did not know any sign language at first, but Clark, the older boy, was able to read lips, so he helped me a lot. Together with Clark, I was able to communicate to the group and give a homily. Eventually, I learned sign language and held a Mass every Sunday for Catholic deaf people at the chapel of St. Anthony's Hospital. We developed a nice community of Catholic and non-Catholic deaf. We had all kinds of social activities, including dances and meetings with the wider deaf community.

I became a regular fixture in the Christensen home. Dorothy was a great cook – a meat, potatoes, and gravy kind of cook. In addition, her husband Elmer worked in an ice cream factory and always had some delicious ice cream for us as dessert. After a meal with the Christensens, I usually took a few turns around the block before heading home – to burn off a few calories, you know!

During dinner it was interesting to watch Dorothy and Clark "talking." Dorothy used her own sign language with special sound affects. One of the things that intrigued me was how she would stamp her foot to break into a conversation. Being with the Christensen boys and our other deaf friends, I learned to appreciate the gift of language and the ability to hear and be heard. We get so used to superficial talk and waste a lot of energy saying nothing. Concrete nouns are one thing, but when it comes to abstract ideas, we hearing people take for granted how easily we can describe a feeling or a thought.

The only downside of my time in the Mississippi Valley was the appearance of serious allergies that would continue to bother me for years to come. My allergy doctor started giving me regular injections. This was the beginning of a not-so-beautiful relationship with the allergy needle.

Spalding Institute - Peoria, Illinois

In 1959, our provincial felt that our house in Rock Island needed a change. I was transferred to Spalding Institute in Peoria, another of the diocese's schools (closed since 1974). Being a good religious, I obediently left Rock Island to take up my new assignment, but it was a sad parting. This was one of the moments in my religious life when I really felt the sacrifice of our vow of obedience. We give up our freedom to set our own course in life. That's not always easy. Sometimes, you think you know better than your superior what is good for you or the community, but you let go of what you think and you obey. I did not want to leave Rock Island. I loved what I was doing, and I loved the people there. But above all that, I wanted to follow the Lord: "Not my will, but yours be done."

Spalding Institute, an all boys school, was originally staffed by the Benedictines. The "Benes," as we affectionately called them, despite their reputation for running schools, apparently did not have much control over the students at Spalding. It was said that the students used to hang one of the teachers by the legs outside a second story window – only when they were bored, of course.

I spent five years at Spalding Institute, from 1959 to 1964. The thing I remember most about Peoria was that I disliked it. The whole area disheartened me. I had been spoiled by the congenial climate of Rock Island. I missed my students, the loving Belgian people, my confreres at our faculty house, our good friends among the diocesan clergy, the opportunity of running over to shop in Davenport – all this had been wonderful and I missed it sorely. In Peoria, I made few friends. I never got in touch with the diocesan clergy there because the *Forty Hours Devotion* became an outmoded liturgical celebration.

The atmosphere of the house in Peoria was quite different from the one I had known in Rock Island. I can recall one occasion when the superior came into the TV room at 8:00 P.M. and told all of us teachers to shut off the TV and get up into our rooms and prepare our classes. I was in my thirties, a grown man, and I did not like being treated this way, but I took my vow of obedience seriously. I left for my room.

Spalding Institute was an unpretentious building across the street from the Academy of Our Lady run by the Sisters of St. Joseph. This fact was not wasted on the boys. At lunchtime, the girls would line up and come across the street to the Spalding Institute cafeteria. It really was nothing unusual, but the Spalding boys thought it was the highlight of the day. They would stand in the window watching the parade. It seems that they hadn't seen girls for so long.

I certainly met some interesting characters during my time at Spalding. Brother Robert Schoffman, for example, loved guns. He made his own bullets by putting the gunpowder into the bullet chamber. From time to time, I could hear him firing away in the basement where he had set up his own firing range. He didn't hesitate in the practical application of his hobby, either. After collecting and counting the money at the Spalding home basketball games, he would put on his deputy sheriff badge and head down to the bank to make a deposit. He carried a pistol as well as a Black Jack. God help anyone who tried to rob him.

For a while, Brother Schoffman devoted himself to eliminating the pigeons who were crowding the rafters above the school door. They were a constant nuisance, always littering the steps below. With the help of his air rifle, Brother Schoffman was able to reduce the pigeon population, much to the distress of some of the locals who were upset that a holy brother of the Viatorians would have the hardness of heart to kill God's creatures. The police even got into the act. They told brother that he did not have the right to shoot pigeons in a public area. The carnage ended there. I understand that a steel net of some kind was eventually put up so that the pigeons would not congregate above the steps.

Despite his fascination with firearms, Brother Schoffman was a noted biologist and ichthyologist, a fish expert, who worked with the Academy of Science at Reelfoot Lake, Tennessee. He spent every summer at a federal research project in Tennessee. He was involved in an investigation of the effect of nuclear waste on fish life in the area where a nuclear project was being proposed.

Animals figure in another memory of mine from these years in Peoria. Some of us Viatorian priests who taught at

Spalding Institute used to help out at a church in Pekin, Illinois, just across the Illinois River, south of Lake Peoria. The pastor there was a nice man, very tall and lanky. I enjoyed going over there to say Mass on weekends. I had quite a shock, however, the first time I was invited into the rectory for coffee. I discovered that the house had not one, but about thirty cats running all over the place, on the floor, on the sofa, on the stairs, and even on the table where we were having coffee. No way was I going to stay for breakfast! None of the priests who went there on weekends to say Mass ever stayed for a meal. We all referred to the rectory, albeit affectionately, as the "cat" house.

Towards the end of my time at Spalding, we began to see some changes in the Church as a result of the Second Vatican Council. The greatest, of course, was the saying of Mass in the vernacular. Never having been a fan of Latin, I wasn't complaining. A smaller item was the change in our habit. During the Spalding days, we gradually stopped wearing the long cassocks and began to wear shirts and trousers with suit coats or sweaters. A great relief. All during my years at Alleman High School we wore the long cassocks with a cord tied around the waist. They were never really practical. They took too much time to put on in the morning and were dangerous: you could get them caught on a chair or something and fall.

During my final days in Peoria, we saw the first of what would become an exodus of our priests. One of our Viatorians feigned drowning off Rehoboth Beach, Virginia. His girlfriend met him some miles down the coast, and they drove out to California to set up house. His plan would have worked if he hadn't returned to Chicago to tell his mother that he was still alive. That was how we found out about him. This was a typical "sixties" story.

To keep my sanity while in Peoria, I found various projects. I accepted a commission to be editor of the religious communities' section of *The Catholic Encyclopedia for Home and School Use* published by McGraw Hill. I spent a good deal of time working on this project and received a check for $700.00, which I turned over to the community. I also stayed busy keeping my book *The Guide to the Catholic Sisterhoods* up to date.

By far my greatest lifeline during the Peoria days was the Christensen family. I didn't have a car to go see them, but I could jump on the train that ran from Chicago through Peoria, Rock Island, Galesburg, and St. Louis. One of the boys would pick me up and bring me back to the station the next day. I would stay in the Viatorian faculty house at Alleman High School and arrange to say Mass at St. Anthony's Hospital for all the deaf people who could attend. Then, I would visit Dorothy and Elmer for dinner . . . and ice cream. Instead of walking around the block to work dinner off, I would walk up and down the platform while I waited for my train. I did this once a month for the five years I was in Peoria.

The allergies I had begun to suffer with in Rock Island grew progressively worse in Peoria. Technically, my condition was called sinusitis. My difficulty breathing kept me awake all night sometimes. I managed to survive five years in Peoria with these allergies. I can remember one day leaving the doctor's office, going down in the elevator, and then feeling faint at the bottom floor. I went right back up to the doctor's office and – what do you think? After giving me some adrenaline to revive me, he wanted to give me an extra dose of pollen shots. I said no way.

I heard that Wisconsin, the state right above Illinois, had less ragweed than the mighty Mississippi Valley, so I spent that August and September at a parish church there. It helped a little. Then I heard Las Vegas, Navada had no ragweed at all. That sounded like heaven to me. I applied to work there and my request was granted. I was transferred to Bishop Gorman High School in the Diocese of Las Vegas. The transfer was a relief in more ways than one.

Bishop Gorman – Las Vegas, Nevada

I spent nine happy years at Bishop Gorman, from 1964 to 1973. First of all, I loved the climate. For a northeasterner, sunshine is a treat. I was greedy for all I could get. The nearby church had a pool we were invited to use at any time, so I was a frequent visitor. Secondly, the faculty and families at Bishop Gorman were great. I made a lot of good friends when I joined the parent-teacher bowling team that met on Sunday evenings. Gorman parents did not expect too much from us. All they wanted was that we give their sons and daughters a good Catholic education and discipline them according to what we thought was right and just. We tried to do that. Bishop Gorman was co-ed with about 600-700 students at that time. (I didn't mind teaching in a co-ed school, but I have to say from my own experience that co-ed schools make things a bit more difficult. The girls tend to work hard and the boys kind of lay back. In an all-boys school, you get better competition from the boys.)

For awhile, I was chaplain for the Gorman High School football team. This meant that I led the football team and staff in a little prayer before the games. I can't say that my tenure as chaplain was very successful. We never won a championship, or even got close, in spite of the fact that we had one of the greatest quarterbacks in the history of Gorman High. His name was David Humm. I had both David and his brother Tommy Humm in class – both super gentlemen, as well as extraordinary athletes. In his senior year, David had the pick of any college team in the country. Even Notre Dame was interested in him. He chose the Red Necks in Nebraska and did so well there that the Los Angeles Raiders drafted him later. David was with the Raiders when they won the Super Bowl championship. Some time later, I ran into Dave while I was visiting his father in the hospital and he showed me his huge Super Bowl championship ring.

I also served as golf and tennis coach at Gorman. I knew nothing about either, but you have to be a good religious and do the things that are assigned to you. I learned to play golf and enjoyed it immensely. I loved coaching because I was able to get into the beautiful Sahara Country Club and play for free as long as I went with the golf team. I didn't have much actual coaching to do. Most of the boys were better golfers than I was. My main job was to make sure they obeyed the rules of the course and didn't get into trouble. During my time as golf coach, I also started the Gorman girls' golf team.

Another athletic service I gave at Gorman was overseeing admission collections at the football, basketball, and wrestling matches. During the home basketball games, I could count on John Heigel to be at my side. All I had to do was give him a call and he would be there. He spent hours collecting and counting out the basketball admission. John worked for the federal government as a scientist in Boulder City. He had the physique of a man who could play professional football; yet, he was a kind and sensitive person. The one thing I remember most about him was the pipe always hanging from his mouth. I don't think he ever really smoked it. John raised three children, one boy and three girls. His son became a priest.

I worked under several principals at Gorman High School, but the one that stands out in my mind and in my heart is Father Edward Anderson who served there from 1966 to 1969. He was also a good friend and my favorite golf partner. During the summer especially, Msgr. Ben Franzenelli and sometimes Msgr. Elwood Lavoy would join Father Ed and me for some early morning golf at the prestigious Desert Inn Golf Club. We clergy played golf "on the house". We only had to pay for use of the golf cart.

During my time in Las Vegas, I was witness to one of the most dramatic financial dilemmas the Catholic Church in this country has ever known. Bishop Joseph Green was the Ordinary of the Diocese of Las Vegas when I first arrived at Gorman. He was a gentle, kind man, who tended to be at the mercy of his own clergy. Along with the La Salette Fathers, Bishop Green made a bad investment that lost millions for the diocese. He couldn't handle the situation and was replaced by Bishop Norman McFarland, a financial expert and canon lawyer. Bishop McFarland's imposing physical stature matched his interior disposition. He demanded absolute obedience from his priests – and got it. We nicknamed him "Absolute Norm." The story goes that the federal government told Bishop McFarland that if the money was not replaced by Good Friday at noon the government would close down the Diocese of Las Vegas which then included the whole state of Nevada. That meant everything-churches, schools, hospitals – anything the Church was running. Bishop McFarland was able to secure the necessary funds by writing letters to all the dioceses and religious communities in the United States. Eventually, he paid off the debt to all the groups that gave him money. I was there when they burned the debt papers. I don't know how many people were aware of the magnitude of this event. It would have meant the loss of the entire state of Nevada for the Catholic Church.

I thought I would escape pollen in Las Vegas, but to my surprise in place of ragweed I found black olive and mulberry trees. Just as lethal! I went to see an allergy doctor, and he started giving me shots in each arm every week. No fun. One day, I had a severe reaction to the shots and had to be rushed over to the doctor's office. I think I almost died on his table. He looked scared. This experience was followed by a visit to the cardiologist who informed me that I had atrial fibrillation. I would be on medication for the rest of my life.

Nosebleeds have also plagued me since my time in Las Vegas. My right nostril seems to have some weak cells; it will start to bleed for no apparent reason. Once when I was driving, the blood began to stream out unexpectedly. I had to hold onto my nose with the left hand and drive with my right. I was afraid I would get into an accident. I drove to the nearest emergency room and had my nose clamped. It stopped bleeding after awhile. Another time, I had a nose bleed just before I was to go out golfing with Father Ed Anderson. I got an emergency appointment with Dr. Donald Romeo, a good friend and the Gorman athletic team doctor. He looked frightened when he saw me – though I don't know why he should have been: at that time he was the official ring doctor for the fights in Las Vegas. I would have thought he was used to the sight of blood. In any case, he cauterized my nose and I went out and played eighteen holes of golf. Another time, I was offering the Mass on a Sunday morning and my nose started bleeding between the first and second readings. Fortunately, I had by this time learned to travel with some cotton balls in my pocket, so I was able to save my parishioners from a grisly scene, not to mention keep from staining my white chasuble.

At Gorman, I also realized a significant loss in my hearing. I noticed that I had difficulty hearing students at the back of the classroom. I knew I had perforated eardrums, but I had never given it much attention. My confreres kidded me about not being able to hear, but you know how it goes: those of us who having hearing problems don't want to admit it. We let the years fly by without doing anything about it. I finally made an appointment with Dr. Howard House of the House Ear Clinic located in St. Vincent's Medical Center, Los Angeles, California. Dr. House examined me and told me I needed an operation. The procedure has a fancy name, but essentially what he did was take a piece of skin and fold it over the part of the ear that was perforated. The surgery was a success, so I had the other ear done the following year. I got back about seventy percent of my hearing in the right ear and about sixty percent in the left ear. Dr. House never even charged me for his services. He asked only that I pray for the success of his clinic and the good hearing of his patients.

(Years later, I broke down and decided to get hearing aids, too. None of us want to wear hearing aids. It makes us look old. But if we compare them to glasses, what's really the difference? I have been wearing hearing aids so long now that I don't realize it anymore. I'm sure that this little sacrifice of my vanity has helped me in my relationships and in my work. I can't be an effective priest if I can't hear.)

Between the atrial fibrillation and the nose bleeding and the problems with my hearing, I was really coming face to face with my mortality for the first time. It may seem strange that a nosebleed could be so traumatic for someone, but if you have ever had the experience of blood just running out of your body with no stopping, you will understand why it shook me up so much. I started to realize my fragility as a human being. One minute we are doing fine, and the next we are face to face with eternity.

You may wonder if I got into gambling while I was in Las Vegas. I'm afraid I have nothing exciting to tell you. My mother, on the other hand, was a big bingo fan. When she came out to see me, I hooked her up with Viatorian Father George Harris's mother to take her out for a little bingo. She liked to gamble, though she hated to lose money. For my part, gambling had no allure. I hated to see my money go down the drain with a quick pull of a "one-armed bandit" (slot machine). On those occasions when I did go to a casino, my philosophy was to take just ten dollars with me and then try my luck. Sometimes I would be able to play with these ten dollars for an hour or so before the machine ate up my money.

Without a doubt, the people I knew in Las Vegas were the real reason for my happiness there.

Catherine and Luke Mullen were among my closest friends in Las Vegas. Luke worked as a pharmacist while Catherine served Our Lady of Las Vegas Elementary School for thirty years as secretary and jack of all trades. Catherine had three children from a previous marriage. Her son, Dan Nolan, became a Viatorian priest. On many occasions, I dined at the Mullens with Fathers Bibeault, Anderson, and Father Dan. Sometimes Father Dan's sister Cathy and his brother Bill and his wife Linda would join us. Not only was Catherine Mullen one of the most loved and appreciated woman at Our Lady of Las Vegas, she was also a gourmet chef and attentive hostess. She made sure we always had our favorite drinks and a good supply of hors d'oeuvres. She would pop her head in every once in a while to see if we were being treated properly. Father Dan would assure her that we were. Then, we would sit down to a dinner that always began with soup du jour, followed usually by Catherine's famous pot roast, candied potatoes, and sweetened carrots. After dinner, we were guided into the living room for some cordial. After a half-hour or so, Catherine would offer us some fruit or prepare my favorite dessert, Boston cream pie. Then we would enjoy our final drink of the evening. People like Catherine Mullen make life beautiful.

Jeanne Sheehan, Cathy, and her husband, the late Joe Sheehan, were friends of the Viatorians long before I arrived in Las Vegas. They were among our "lay-pioneers" who helped our ministry get off the ground. Jeanne could remember that fateful day when St. Viator Church began to crumble. Father Crowley, C.S.V., had warned the bishop that the intended site for the church was unstable ground, but his words went unheeded. He was ordered to continue with the building project. The church was finished in September and began falling apart during the Christmas season. Eventually it had to be torn down. The tension that this situation created between Father Crowley and the bishop eventually led to father's dismissal from the diocese. He did not leave quietly. He made the front page of *Time Magazine* and was given a week's round of parties by all his friends in the hotels and casinos in Las Vegas. Father Crowley had won the affection and appreciation of the Las Vegas crowd by saying Mass in the Flamingo Hotel at 3:00 A.M. for the entertainers who finished their work around 2:30 A.M.

Father Crowley was followed by Father Pat Toomey, C.S.V., who saw to the construction of the present Guardian

Angel Shrine which began life as a humble "mission" church in 1963 before it assumed the status of a cathedral for the newly created Diocese of Las Vegas-Reno. Hotel owners donated money to the project so that a beautiful church would be available for visitors to Las Vegas. In fact, this unique parish can boast that on any given Sunday, seventy-five percent of those attending Mass are tourists. Jeanne Sheehan helped organize and pick out the furniture and other incidentals to beautify the church building. She and Cathy Sheehan are still faithful participants in parish life there.

I also made good friends with Rae and Phil Reinhart. I had their oldest boy Mike in class. Rae's mother, Adelaide, took a liking to me, too, and we got along very well. Whenever the family had something to celebrate, they always invited me over. Without a doubt, the Reinharts made my fiftieth birthday party the greatest of my life. It started with my complete surprise. All my friends and colleagues were invited. There was liquor galore, and the pool table was covered with food made by the chefs at Caesar's Palace where Phil worked as a maintenance engineer. Phil even had one of the artists at Caesar's Palace draw a huge caricature of me playing golf.

I have to pause for a moment and talk about the changes taking place around this time in the Church. I was a first hand witness to the events that followed the Second Vatican Council. I had grown up and studied for the priesthood in the pre-conciliar church. I lived through the confusion and sorrow that came in the wake of the council: the exodus of religious – including large numbers of my own brother Viatorians – and the emergence of two kinds of Catholicism in this country.

No topic has been so charged as the question of the Latin Mass. I remember that my good friend Dorothy Christensen in Rock Island was all for keeping the Latin. For my part, I loved the Latin Mass, but I could also see the pastoral need for the vernacular. When I hear people complaining about the loss of Latin, it seems to me that what they really miss is the mysterious sound of Latin that made them feel like they were in church. They don't really want Latin because of solid doctrinal or pastoral reasons. It's something old and pretty, like a painting or a statue that they want us to preserve for its own sake. But liturgical life is for the glory of God and the salvation of men; it doesn't exist as an art treasure for its own sake.

The changes I witnessed during my years at Gorman were indications of a great cultural revolution taking place in our country and our Catholic way of life. Gradually, I saw the spirit of these times creeping into the lives of my students. The sixties and seventies undid the traditional values with which I had grown up. My students were like a thermometer on which I could read the state of our religious values. To my dismay, I discovered that many of them were not taking their religious beliefs seriously. They were not even going to Mass on Sunday. The religious instruction I was trying to give them was nothing more than a game.

I began to feel that I was wasting my time. I felt discouraged and wondered if after so many years in the classroom I was just getting stale. Thinking it might be a good time to try another kind of priestly service, I asked my provincial for a change of assignment. I was anxious to try my hand at parish ministry.

An Encountered Priest

In response to my request for parish work, Father Ed Anderson, my provincial at the time, asked me to be pastor at Our Lady of Wisdom Church, Reno, Nevada. I stayed there for three years, from 1973 to 1976.

Our Lady of Wisdom Church was built in gothic style, though the thing I remember most about it was the leaky roof we couldn't afford to repair. We priests lived in a small but comfortable ranch-type house a mile or two from the church. The little bit of distance kept us away from the hustle and bustle of the University of Reno campus located right across the street from the church. Hoards of students were forever walking back and forth over church property. On the other hand, there were some advantages to having a prestigious university on your front lawn. With the help of Nevada Chief Justice John Mowbray, (died 1997) I was able to get two of my former students into the pre-med program. John traveled all the way from Las Vegas every Monday to attend to his duties in the Nevada House of Justice in Reno, and then returned the 500 miles to his wife and family every Friday night. He was a staunch Catholic from the old school. Every time he came to receive communion he pointed his finger to say, "On the tongue."

Father Jack Linnan, C.S.V., was already at Our Lady of Wisdom when I arrived, but his work with the University of

Reno Spiritual Life Center kept him too busy to see to the needs of the parish. Father Jack is one of our order's great intellectuals. He graduated from the famous University of Louvain in Belgium. I was not up to giving a homily to all those intellectuals from the university who attended our church, so I leaned on Father Jack to take the 10:00 A.M. Mass on Sunday. Eventually, Father Jack accepted a professorship at the Catholic Theological Union, at that time – June 1974 – the largest Catholic seminary in the United States. He was replaced at Our Lady of Wisdom by Father Bob Foster, C.S.V.

In taking over as pastor at Our Lady of Wisdom, I was once again jumping into something with no preparation. I really should have taken a special introductory course: "Parish Pastoring 101." Most priests can't wait to be pastors. Usually, they have served as assistant pastors long enough to crave the exercise of their own authority. Having never been an assistant pastor, I didn't have this desire. To me, being a pastor was no big deal – just another way of living my priestly vocation. In my innocence, I expected holy orders and good will to be enough. It wasn't.

One night, during a parish council meeting, I was shocked to realize that some of my parishioners were not happy with me. In fact, the president of the parish council was the ringleader of a movement to have me ousted. He took the occasion to announce that the council wanted me fired. (To make matters worse, my provincial, Father Ken Morris, just happened to be staying with me in the rectory at that time and was in attendance at this meeting.)

I was astonished. Up to that moment, I had believed I was doing a good job. It was a rude awakening. Evidently, the parishioners felt that I didn't care about them because the three previous pastors used to go around visiting them in their homes. I had failed to keep up this practice. The truth was that I had nothing against visiting parishioners – hadn't I enjoyed the hospitality of many friends where I had previously been stationed? The reason I did not make house calls in Reno was that the five previous Viatorians who served in the parish had all fallen in love with female parishioners. All of them eventually left the priesthood and got married. I had no intention of going down the same road!

One of the parishioners, a lawyer and a powerful man in the council, stood up for me and said that he thought I was doing a good job. The matter was ended there, but the stigma remained. I did not know what to do about it. This was my first experience in a parish and as a pastor. I suppose I was just not prepared to assume the responsibility. The atmosphere of that particular parish as an academic community probably also contributed to my difficulties. I recognized the fact that I was not the most intelligent person in the world. I knew I had difficulty getting by in college and in the seminary, and I didn't have the background for the intellectual way of life of my people at Our Lady of Wisdom. Whatever the reason, I felt that I had failed in my role as pastor.

Shortly after this episode, on a day I was feeling particularly down in the mouth, Father George Wolf, principal of Bishop Manogue High School in Reno, invited me to attend an information night for Worldwide Marriage Encounter. He explained that Marriage Encounter could be really helpful to priests by giving them a better understanding of what marriage is about. For my part, I didn't think I needed any group of lay people instructing me on marriage. Nevertheless, I tagged along with Father Wolf to the meeting which was held at a home of one of the Marriage Encounter couples.

I listened to the various sharings, letting them go in one ear and out the other. From my lofty position as ordained minister, I looked down on these couples. They didn't know what they were talking about, I thought. I had spent four years in the seminary at Catholic University of America. I had studied the theology of marriage. I had twenty-two years as a priest under my belt. I thought I knew it all. I just wanted to get out of that house and away from these pressing couples. As soon as I could make my exit as politely as possible, I headed for the door. But I made one mistake. In my haste, I signed a registration blank for something.

A week or so later, I received a notice in the mail that I had been signed up for the September 1974 Marriage Encounter weekend in Sacramento, California.

Of course, I wasn't going to go, but when I mentioned it to Father Bob Foster, who had by that time replaced Father Jack, he was adamant that I should try it. He himself had made a Marriage Encounter weekend and he knew what it was all about. I reached for an excuse: I couldn't go because I had to take care of the Masses at the parish that weekend. Father Bob then proceeded to pull the rug out from under my feet. He would take care of all the Masses. Alas, I had no excuse not to go.

The weekend certainly didn't get off to a glorious start. It was held in the dormitory of a boys' school while the students were away for the weekend. What an atmosphere! The room I was assigned had a lot of girly pictures hanging on the wall. What had I got myself into? I sat down to the first conference feeling torn between staying and leaving.

Why was I here? What could these people tell me that I didn't already know?

I had a lot to learn. The first thing to touch me was the warm welcome I received from the host couple. I was going to be touched again and again over that weekend by this simple human tenderness. I was also introduced to a Marriage Encounter dialogue technique that begins with a "letter." While couples write this letter to each other, we priests write it to God. During this exercise, something opened up in my heart. I discovered my thirst for a greater love of God and my people. The Saturday afternoon talk on death had me weeping profusely. I have been weeping ever since – good tears.

By the end of the weekend, I knew that I wanted to continue with Marriage Encounter, but I wasn't sure how that would be possible. Then the host couple asked me if I would be interested in being a priest for Marriage Encounter, to serve with the presenting teams that give weekends. I couldn't believe I was being asked to join this incredible ministry. I have always had a poor image of myself and my abilities. Particularly at that time, with all the criticism I was getting in the parish, I had no confidence in myself. I knew that learning and studying was very hard for me. I knew I wasn't a flamboyant speaker. I simply felt that I had nothing to offer. But Marriage Encounter wanted me. They believed that I could give something valuable to couples.

Marriage Encounter

God bless Father Wolf for seeking me out and dragging me to that first meeting. God bless Father Bob for not accepting my flimsy excuses. Although I couldn't have known it at the time, their insistence probably saved my priesthood.

By the time Marriage Encounter came into my life, I had been in holy orders for twenty-two years. I loved being a priest and wanted to be a priest to the fullest extent possible. Marriage Encounter became for me the way to do this. For nearly thirty years now, I have been a presenting priest with this movement. I can't emphasize enough the role Marriage Encounter has played in my life as a human being and a priest. I have known many other priests who didn't find a way to grow in their vocation. They ended up leaving the ministry. I wonder what would have been the outcome if they had had the chance to experience their priesthood in the context of Marriage Encounter as I did. I am certain that the Holy Spirit inspired Father Wolf to invite me to that first meeting, and then inspired Father Bob to urge me to go.

As I mentioned elsewhere, the most important thing for me is relationship. I have always loved and been there for my blood family, but the difficult circumstances of our life together and the fact that I spent most of my adult years far away meant that I didn't find in this natural relationship a really sustaining bond. Nor was I ever able to make such a tie in my religious life, although I loved and respected my brother Viatorians greatly. Marriage Encounter filled this gap for me. I love working with people who are interested in growing in relationship; I love finding ways to make the contact between people more intimate, more solid.

Father Gabriel Calvo first developed Marriage Encounter in Spain in the 1950s. Its success eventually gave the movement the designation "worldwide." The goal of Marriage Encounter is to help couples who already have good marriages enrich their relationship with one another, their families, and God. At the same time, Marriage Encounter can also provide couples in difficulty with an opportunity to rediscover their love for one another. Couples are invited to attend a weekend presented by a team of three couples and a priest, usually in a hotel, and according to a fixed, carefully planned program. During an encounter weekend, couples discuss privately such topics as intimacy, finances, their relationship with the Church, self-awareness, fears that inhibit openness, and the spirituality of marriage.

Marriage Encounter weekends demand a lot of time, work, preparation, and prayer. The weekend itself is only the tip of the iceberg. Hardly anyone is aware of the hours of labor that go into the weekend's fourteen talks: getting them written and workshopped before they are finally accepted. You cannot be a presenter unless you go through this process. It sometimes takes weeks, months, even as much as a year to get a presentation approved for a weekend. All talks must be brought in line with the Marriage Encounter outline and ideology. We are not allowed to go off the written word, either. This is to insure that the talks given at each Marriage Encounter weekend are the same throughout the world.

Each weekend follows a tight, carefully prepared program. On Friday night, we emphasize the importance of feelings. On Saturday, we review the various phases which ordinary couples go through together. Then, on Sunday, we try to highlight the importance of God in the matrimonial relationship. We talk about celibacy at this point. The priest is not the only one committed to celibacy. Couples are committed to it in terms of their fidelity to each other. How about that?

In my opinion, my talks are not that great, but it seems that my lack of oratory skill is more than compensated for by my sensitivity. That is a fancy way of saying that I cry easily. Evidently, I have touched a lot of couples on weekends simply because I can open up on an emotional level. Couples feel that I empathize with them, so they are not afraid to approach me. Also, I think that showing my sensitive side helps many couples learn something about the priesthood that they never knew: that priests are human, too. I'm sure that after a weekend they go back to their parishes with a different attitude towards their priest back home.

I know of at least one young man whose perspective on the priesthood changed radically because of my sharing during a weekend. I was in Phoenix at the time. Just before we concluded our final meal together, the executive couple asked if we would listen to one of the husbands who wanted to say a few words to the group. This young man got up and addressed himself to me in front of everyone, thanking me for coming all the way from Chicago, and specifically for the sharings I had given on Friday night and all day Saturday. He said that he never knew priests were human, or that they had feelings and insecurities, too. I had really helped him understand better not only the role of a priest, but also the importance of his Catholic faith. When he was finished, we gave each other a big hug with all the other couples applauding around us.

As I mentioned, one activity during a Marriage Encounter weekend is the writing of a letter. Couples write these letters to each other and the presenting priest writes his letter to God. I remember one weekend: I looked up from my writing and saw all these men, some sitting or lying facedown on the floor, busily writing their letters to their wives. One husband I noticed was wringing his right hand to relieve the cramps from writing so fast. What a sight! People would be amazed to discover just how much men have in their hearts for their wives. Somehow, over time, these feelings get buried. Given the opportunity and a little push, however, out they come tumbling over each other.

This is the secret of Marriage Encounter: it helps people break through to feelings they have forgotten or sometimes don't even know they possess. It helps them to get these sentiments out in the open so that real solutions can be found. As one man said after the Phoenix weekend, "I am the quiet type and I am afraid to show my feelings. But this weekend has been a moment of truth in our married life. We are being more open and honest with each other." A wife on that weekend said that she and her husband had been married ten years but had had no real conversation for the last three. She also told the team that they had been married by a justice of the peace, but the following May planned to be married in the Catholic Church. Another couple confided to us that though they had only been married five months, they were very happy to have made this weekend so early in their married life.

Thanks to Marriage Encounter, and my work with similar movements such as Retrouvaille and Beginnings Experience, I have experienced first hand the liberation that we offer couples. But this liberation is not restricted only to the couples on an encounter weekend.

Up until just a few years ago, I continued to carry the burden of hatred in my heart for my father. Sometimes this showed itself in odd ways. I hate cucumbers, for example. One day when I was a youngster, my father got mad at me because I wouldn't eat the cucumbers he had put on my plate. I just didn't like them. He tried to make me eat them. I would not. The more he insisted, the more I resisted. It was an ugly scene. To this day, every time I see or smell cucumbers, I feel sick. I pick them out of my salads. I know that they are good, healthy food, but because of my problems with my father, I can't even look at them.

Cucumbers were the least of my problems. I went through my priesthood harboring this hatred for my father. What I didn't realize was how much my hardness of heart affected all my relationships. By refusing to forgive my father, I was holding up a barrier between God and myself, not to mention the people in my life. Somehow, this wall had to come down.

In the 1980s, I became involved with the Beginnings Experience movement for widowed and divorced people. While I was workshopping my talks, I described my resentment towards my father. The team leaders reminded me that I had to forgive my dad; I couldn't be going around preaching forgiveness to others and telling them in confession to forgive their neighbor when I was holding back towards my father. I took this advice to heart. On that weekend, participants wrote a letter to their spouses, whether living or dead, as a way of healing their relationships psychologically. I wrote my letter to my father. I apologized to him for the forgiveness I had withheld for years and years. I was finally able to let go of my bitterness and close the chapter on my hatred.

I have learned a lot about marriage in my years with Marriage Encounter. I have seen that the biggest challenge facing married couples in this world today is staying in touch with each other. After a wonderful, romantic wedding, the routine of life gets a hold of them and they lose each other. They start to take each other for granted. They forget to say

"I love you" every day. Husbands will tell me, "My wife knows that I love her. I don't need to say it everyday." Wrong. They do. Their wives need to hear it again and again. It makes them feel safe; it makes them feel that their husbands are keeping the vows they made on their wedding day. And the second challenge is similar: continuing to have respect for each other. Expressions like "the old bag" or "housekeeper" have no place in everyday conversation. Nor do nagging sentences that begin, "You always . . ." or "You never . . ." Couples must also learn not to interrupt each other.

It's funny, I know, that we need to be reminded of these things which are so simple, but in many cases a marriage will stand or fall on just this kind of behavior. Just consider what this wife wrote to me after she and her husband made a weekend:

> I want to thank you for this very special weekend . . . what an eye-opening experience we had. You have opened the door to happiness in our household again. My husband realized that after seventeen years of marriage, I still need him just as much as I did the day I married him. I've always tried to make this point to him, but somehow, he didn't understand. The Marriage Encounter weekend helped him to feel again – actually feel alive and in love again. I used to wake up every morning thinking how I can get out of this marriage, but with three children and responsibilities I found no solution. Thank God, I stayed because now I go to sleep and wake up with peace in my heart.

Marriage Encounter works. If it didn't, I wouldn't have stuck around so long. Though we do not provide a panacea for all difficulties, we do offer couples the tools to make their marriage deeper and stronger. There's no magic formula, however. Couples have to cooperate; they have to do their share of the work. It is like going to the dentist. You can't be relieved of the toothache if you don't open your mouth. If couples listen and accept what we have to give them, they can take control of the situations in their marriage that are preventing them from living a full, happy married life. Even though arguments are inevitable in every human relationship, if a couple learns to communicate they can prevent these flare-ups from developing into really serious fights. They can learn to stop, look and listen with their hearts.

One of my cherished letters – of the hundreds I possess from over thirty years in Marriage Encounter – beautifully describes how one wife evolved during a weekend:

> When John and I arrived Friday evening at the Sheraton, I looked around to try and figure out who were the team couples . . . When I saw your nametag on your Hawaiian shirt, I said to myself, "He can't be the Marriage Encounter priest. He looks too gruff – surely, he won't know anything about me or how I'm feeling." I felt smug in a way. I was hurting and desperately lonely because John and I had grown so far apart. But I knew I was "tough" and could go on and live my own life if I had to as what I later found out is called a "married single."
>
> As you know, the Smiths went through the "housekeeping chores" – the rules, the regulations

and so on, of the weekend, and I felt a little of the "ho-hum" feeling. Your joking around reminded me of some of the kindergarten board meetings, when I would clown around a little. I knew you were a little uncomfortable and were trying to break the ice, but I just couldn't let go of my masks.

But you and the Smiths kept saying, "Trust us . . . go with it . . . don't be an observer at the weekend . . . give it a chance." The more you said it, the more I was able to believe you.

Later, as you showed us more of your feelings and your vulnerable side, I could see pieces of my own father and I wanted to reach out and cry and hug you. And I felt sad because I know no priests who have given me the gift to see their inside emotions. How much better all those Sundays in Mass would have been if I knew. Thank you for sharing yourself with us. The weekend wouldn't have been the same without your input, your help, your obvious love and concern. The analogy of how you and the Smiths were feeling like parents just before Christmas morning was special. All of us with children can relate so well to those feelings. It wasn't really until I had children myself, and could love them so deeply and have such hopes for them (and yet be angry, too, and want to shake them at times) – that I began to understand God's love for his people. I grew up as a Catholic and went to Mass regularly, but I didn't know why until I had children. By feeling that emotion – all those emotions – I began to understand on an infinitesimal level God's love for me and all people.

During one of my talks with John, I told him my relationship with my religion is sort of like a Marriage Encounter on an ongoing basis. (He has only known that I feel guilty when I don't go to Mass; and to him the only reason for me to go was to keep from feeling guilty.) But I was able to compare [going to Mass] with this weekend.

Often, when John and I would talk in the room, the phone would ring and call us back. And we would sigh and say we wished we could continue our time of discussion. But we knew we wanted to go back because another presentation would give us more food for thought. It would give us another seed to sow. We could continue again after the presentation. For me, Mass is like that. Often I would like to finish reading the newspaper on Sunday morning. But I sigh and say I need to go to Mass. Like at the Marriage Encounter presentations, I don't always hear every word of every Mass because a seed may be planted and my mind follows that idea for a few minutes before tuning back in. But the act of being present, with others, is a statement. I felt good, Father, being able to explain this to John in this way. I had never fully crystallized it in my own mind before the weekend. For me, ever since we were in high school, it has been an area I couldn't explain logically; so therefore it was taboo.

There was one other thought which I wanted to share with you. On Sunday afternoon, a fear –

almost a panicky feeling – crept over me. I imagined a fragile spider web, still wet with dew, very new and very fresh. Now I was being asked to transfer that precious web to another spot. It was so beautiful, so perfect where it was. How could I possibly do this without ruining it?

The answer came with the prayer couples and Mass. I could see in my mind a sturdier network – one that could be superimposed on my fragile web. One that would "fix" each strand as we transferred it to our home. Knowing we won't be left alone has been a real gift to me. (Now, too, I understand the gift of the Holy Spirit. God did not leave us alone either after the personal encounter Jesus had on earth.) Amazing; and I didn't think this was supposed to be a religious weekend. I've learned so much.

People will sometimes ask how a priest can help in a troubled marriage. What does he know about being married? I can tell you that the presence of a priest on a Marriage Encounter weekend is not just a pretty decoration. It can be salvific for a marriage.

The Marriage Encounter logo is two hearts entwined together with the cross of Jesus Christ. The priest is present on a weekend because he represents God in the matrimonial contract. Marriage is more than just two people shacking up together; it is a sacrament. The presence of the priest is a way of saying that you have made your vows in the sight of God and His people. This is no light matter. We are here now to help you keep your relationship together and make it stronger. What we have witnessed, we now seek to serve. Couples can use the priest to recover the real meaning of their marriage – over and above all the peripheral issues that tend to weigh down their situation.

Let me give you an example. In September of this year, I attended a weekend in which a young couple left early. They just walked out the door without telling anyone that they were going. We on the team were sorry to see them go. A week later, however, I received a call from the husband. He was desperate. He came to my house and we had a good talk, during which he was crying about the fact that his wife had separated from him. She had agreed to go on the Marriage Encounter weekend, but they had failed to really get into it. I listened to him and gradually it became clear that he and his wife were essentially "married singles." They were each doing their own thing. On top of that, both were drinking. I invited him to return with his wife. They came together, and after awhile the wife agreed to give her husband another chance. They would go to see a counselor and then perhaps make a Retrouvaille weekend for troubled couples. All of this came to pass because they were touched by my presence at the weekend. It made a difference for them that a priest was there.

One of the greatest things for a priest in Marriage Encounter is the gratitude and confidence that he receives from the couples. Our presence among them lifts them up; in turn, their appreciation lifts us up and brings the priest out of us. We are really "father" to our couples. I have hundreds of letters and cards from the couples I have met on Marriage Encounter weekends. These are among my greatest personal treasures. I take them out and read them when I need a burst of encouragement. They tell me more than anything else that my life hasn't been in vain:

"We don't know where to begin other than to say that our marriage has changed a great deal already. If someone would have told us a week ago that our marriage would be this good after our weekend, I would not have believed them! A year ago our marriage was at the lowest point it had been. We agreed to see a marriage counselor and noticed an improvement after a few sessions, but there was still something missing. Almost every fight was about the same thing . . . If we had already seen a marriage counselor, what was left? Our Marriage Encounter weekend was the answer to our prayers. It was your presentations and God's presence that unlocked the door to our feelings. Without that we would be where we were a week ago. We never want to go back there! Thank you for sharing your experiences with us and thank you for sharing your LOVE!"

"I want to thank you so much for being vulnerable to us this weekend, although I suspect that this is the way you are all the time. Thank you for teaching us that priests are human, sensitive and vulnerable. You touched my heart like no one else has done in a long time. I feel blessed sharing this weekend with you, getting to know you and getting to love you . . . To me, it is as if the Lord placed you in our midst, just so that He would have the best representative possible."

"What a privilege it has been to share in your life on our very special weekend. You are not only a joy to be with, but you have been very much an inspiration to both of us with your deep trust in us and your gift of sensitivity. Having a priest like you, and as you have been to us here this weekend, fills our hearts with such true thankfulness to our Lord for allowing our paths to cross, and to share intimately in each other's lives. We try never to take our encounter with men like you for granted as just 'a priest we met on a weekend,' but rather, to carry you in our hearts and our prayers as a special dear friend from this day forward . . . We guess 'Thank you' is not enough in words to tell you how appreciative we are for your coming here to be with us, but most of all, what you gave us of who you are."

The satisfaction of knowing that I have made a difference in someone's life gives me life as a priest. I have always struggled with a poor self-image; thanks to Marriage Encounter, I have been able to find something positive about myself – something to celebrate, something for which I could give heartfelt thanks to God. As one of Marriage Encounter's banners says, "God does not make junk."

When I think of the priests I have known who left the priesthood, and there are many, I feel so sad. If they had only had the experience of an Encounter weekend! Perhaps, like me, they could have helped countless couples open up to each other and at the same time fully experience the depth of their own vocation. Lay people don't realize how much they help a priest discover his priesthood by asking him to use the sacred powers he has received. At the end of a Marriage Encounter weekend, the people are always so grateful for the presence of a priest. But it's really the priest that should do the thanking. By allowing themselves to be children, my people allow me to be a father. It's a reciprocal relationship.

A Love Letter

I had hardly begun as a Marriage Encounter priest when I wanted to bail out. I went back home to Reno and began writing my talks to prepare for my first weekend. The following January, the executive Marriage Encounter people changed many of the talks. I had to rewrite many of mine. What a job! I hadn't even given a weekend yet and I already felt like quitting. After writing a talk, I had to go and get it workshopped by a couple – lay people no less (I still had a lot to learn about lay-priest cooperation). They were pretty tough on me. I was writing what I thought was important, but they reminded me that I had to conform to the Marriage Encounter outline. I spent a lot of time going over my talks and rewriting them for my first weekend. Even afterwards, I continued refining my talks over the years. This was another way that Marriage Encounter kept me growing.

I gave my first team priest weekend in September 1975, a year after my own first encounter. I was pretty scared, but since my talks had been approved, I had some confidence. Everything came out fine – the beginning of many happy years with Marriage Encounter.

Despite the success of the weekend, I still had to face the situation back at Our Lady of Wisdom Parish. A year had passed, but I could still feel the tension around me. I was really at a loss for what to do. My one consolation was that I could rely on Father Bob to take the main Masses, and especially to give the homily at the Midnight Mass for

Christmas. I did not feel qualified to give such an important homily, one of the most important of the liturgical year, to a parish of intellectuals. My shortcomings seemed even larger in the face of the criticism that I was getting.

Then, in November, tragedy struck. Father Bob had a heart attack one day while driving back from his exercise program at the local club. He went immediately to the local hospital. All his activities came to a sudden halt. He had to give up his job as chaplain at the Reno University Spiritual Life Center and could no longer help out at the parish. He eventually moved back to Chicago to recuperate and later served many years as a holy priest.

Without Father Bob, what was I going to do? I was left on my own with a parish that evidently had little sympathy for me. And that Christmas homily was staring me in the face: the most public moment of the church year when a priest is supposed to shine for his congregation. I knew that I had to do a good job with this homily because it meant my future in the parish. I didn't want to do it. I was afraid, and this fear snowballed into all kinds of doubts. I felt like quitting, leaving the priesthood and going out into the world. The only problem was that I loved being a priest and didn't want anything to come between me and my vocation. Being pastor of a parish was not equal to being a priest. It was just one way of being a priest. While I loved my people, I really did not care about being a pastor. I knew I could walk away from it, or limp away if I was tossed out.

What was I going to say to my people at Christmas? I needed something more than pious generalities. I spent a good deal of time trying to come up with something. Then all of a sudden it hit me. Why not write my people a love letter, like the kind I had experienced on the Marriage

Encounter weekend? I could tell them how much they meant to me, how sorry I was for whatever inconvenience I had caused them, and promise them that I would try to do better. I would simply open my heart to them and tell them all the things that I was feeling. I poured all this into writing. It was hard, but I was sure that this was the only route left open to me.

The moment finally arrived. I looked up at the congregation and back down at my homily. Trembling, I spoke these words to my people:

The theme of our liturgy this morning is, "Light dispels the darkness." Jesus is the Light that shattered the darkness that had existed in our world for so long. When Jesus came to earth, he . . . made life tolerable, more lovable, and more meaningful. Jesus was born on this day to cast a beam of light, of hope to our world. So, this morning we celebrate that wonderful event in which Jesus turned the darkness of this world around to make it a ray of light and wonderment. Now all of us who live here have been given that ray of light to light up our way to heaven.

Good morning. In the name of Father Bob Foster, who is recuperating from a heart attack, as you all know, and Father Norb Bibeault, who has kindly agreed to help me this weekend, I want to wish you all a very happy and blessed Christmas.

My good friends in Christ, I am writing and reading this love letter to each of you this morning because for the first time in my life, I am learning what love is all about. I have reached the twilight years of my life, and I now can admit that I have learned something about love. Perhaps this is the reason that I never got married, for I was afraid to say, "I love you" to another person, even my mother, God love her.

Yes, I have told the Father in heaven that I love him, and this is easy to do. Whenever you break your promise to God, you can always go to confession and through the power of the priest you can be restored to the good graces of God again.

I want to say to all of you today that I love each one of you and I don't even know you. Yes, I love you. I could not say this a year ago or even a few months ago, but today during my second Christmas among you as your pastor, I can really and truly say that I love you all.

One of the reasons that led to this momentous decision is the fact that you are special people in my life and many of you have revealed to me that I am special to you because of my sacrament of holy orders and what this means to you.

I came among you eighteen months ago, a year last June, as a committed priest and teacher who decided to enter into a new apostolate, a new relationship as pastor of a group of parishioners who were looking for direction and meaning in their spiritual lives. I felt very inadequate when I first arrived at Our Lady of Wisdom because I never had a position of directing and of being responsible for the spiritual direction of others. I knew I wanted change in my lifestyle, but I was afraid that I would not be able to handle all the new responsibilities that a pastor has to face each day. I knew that I had some leadership qualifications, but I have been timid and afraid of becoming a dominant personality.

I realize that I have offended some people in the parish. If they take it as a personal affront then I am sorry, for I have not wanted to offend anyone. My whole philosophy is to make everyone of you love me as I am beginning to love all of you.

Just as the Father in heaven said to his Son, "This is my beloved Son with whom I am well pleased," so I say to all of you this morning, "You are my special people and I love each one of you." Your specialness is the fact that each one of you is a unique creation of God. God made you special and he ordained that you should be with me here during this time of my life.

During this short time that I have been with you at Our Lady of Wisdom, I have grown a lot. I felt that assuming the pastorate of this parish I would get a chance to grow, develop and mature as a priest and pastor. Before I came to Our Lady of Wisdom, I lived in a period of darkness. Now I can tell you that I have grown, I have developed and matured.

I have just been appointed the Vicar of Religious in the northern part of the Diocese of Reno by Bishop Norman McFarland . . . I just published a new edition of my vocational book, "Challenge for Now" . . . and, last September, I made a Marriage Encounter weekend in Sacramento, California where I learned a little something more about marriage . . . And it is you, my people, who made this possible in my life. Thank you.

As I begin the second period of my life as your pastor, I want to make Our Lady of Wisdom a parish that exists for and by the people. It should be a parish oriented to the good of the parishioners. Jesus came to change the world by casting . . . kindness, compassionate love, and mercy, on a world that was full of hatred, greed, and injustice. That is what I want to do. I want to spread a lot of kindness and love and compassion and I want to make Our Lady of Wisdom a place where every parishioner will find love, peace, happiness, and concern for one another.

This is not an impossible dream. I believe that you and I can make it happen. Life should not be boring. We have so many things to do, so many opportunities to explore, so many mountains to climb, so many people that need help and need it now.

Jesus came upon this historical scene and cast a light of hope, enthusiasm, and love which has dissipated the darkness of hatred, greed, and injustice. I hope that all of you here this morning will help me to continue to bring the light of Jesus' message into the lives of all in our parish, especially those who are sick, in pain, living in poverty without the proper food and clothing, those experiencing problems of alcoholism and drugs, those who are widowed or living in home-bound conditions, and everyone who may be living in a quality of life that should not exist in our parish.

Working together, we can help make the beacon of light that Jesus brought to all of us on that first Christmas day, His birthday, into the lives of all our parishioners and make the world of our parish here in Our Lady of Wisdom a better place in which to live, grow, develop, love, and bring up children.

Thank you. May God bless you.

When I reached the end of the homily, the congregation rose to its feet and gave me a thunderous ovation. I could not believe it. My people really loved me. They wanted me. I was not a failure – I was a success! I breathed a prayer of gratitude and relief. Everything was going to be okay.

In February 1975, I received word that my father had passed away in Boston. He had some contact with the family after I left home, but his drinking made full reconciliation impossible. My brother Paul wrote me of my father's last days:

> I can recall when we lived at 917 W. Fourth St., that Ma had our father come home for a little while during the wedding of Terry and Tom. After which, he became a watchman for the wrecking company and the construction of the housing project at "D" Street. He took up drinking again and Ma put him out again, and he went to the South End, and then I think he went into the Merchant Marines, because we lost track of him for quite awhile. I had no contact with him until I got a call from his landlady that he was drinking and busting up the place. I had him over early in my marriage, only once, because he was still drinking and Ginny and I didn't want him around the children. Then, I heard from his landlady about him being sick and went to Long Island Hospital where he passed away.

My father's death left little impression on me. He had died for me so many years before.

As I mentioned in the homily above, I had used my time in Reno to put together another vocations book similar to the one I had done at Catholic University of America. This one was called *Challenge for Now* and was published by Western Printing of Sparks, Nevada. We printed a thousand copies of the book and I mailed them out myself. While I am proud of the finished product, the greatest part of this effort was the friendship I formed with Ted Marston, the publisher. It goes to show how contagious Christianity can be when we just go about our business in faith. In his forward to the book, Mr. Marston, wrote:

> I first met Father Thomas McCarthy early in July 1974, when he came to our office to discuss the publication of this book, which is now an accomplished fact. Father McCarthy had some very definite ideas, or more properly speaking, ideals, about what he wanted the book to accomplish. The idea did not strike me very favorably at the onset, but I was very much intrigued by Father McCarthy, as a person and as a most dedicated compiler and author. He is a most engaging person to converse with, and he has, I believe, almost total communication with people of any genre.

> The upshot of several sessions was that I agreed to publish the book, and I became, in a short time, as dedicated to what the book is intended to accomplish as Father has been. The man is truly tremendous. He has the patience of a saint, and he needed it. We had a most unusual series of happenings in the mechanical departments of our plant that continually threw the publication behind schedule. Yet I never saw any evidence of his being disturbed by this delay in the publication dates . . . There were many hours spent in the mechanics of design for the publication. During

this time I learned a great deal about the modern concept of religious tenets, and the widely accepted practice of all faiths meeting together to create a better understanding of one another.

Father McCarthy's educational qualifications for this book are on the back cover. This does not begin to state the real qualifications that he possesses. Without consciously trying, he has taught me more about what one person can do to make a better world than I had learned in the previous seventy-odd years of my life . . . Knowing Father McCarthy has greatly enriched my life.

Also during my time in Reno, the violin came back into my life – literally. I had given my own violin away at some point. I was tired of carrying it around with me, especially since I never played it anymore. One day, I visited the Carmelite sisters on La Fond Drive in Reno. While speaking with Sister Maria, the prioress, I mentioned that I played the violin. She said that she had a violin to give me, if I would promise to play it. I promised. Being the sort of person I am, I can't make a promise and not follow through. From that day to this, I have practiced my violin consistently. In the last few years, thanks to the encouragement of my friend and accompanist Elaine Doerrfeld, I have been able to bring my talents to local nursing homes and retirement centers during the holidays.

Sabbatical Year: University of California, Berkeley

Though it's true that "All's well that ends well," my time at Our Lady of Wisdom was not the best I had known. I had no problem giving up my pastor's seat when my provincial suggested that I take a sabbatical year starting in June 1976. I had learned I was no pastor, that was for sure! Still, I needed to do something. A year on sabbatical would give me a chance to think about my life and hopefully find a new direction. I was right in step with my times: going on sabbatical was the thing to do in those days. We were smack in the middle of the turbulence following Vatican Council II. Priests were leaving left and right – sisters and nuns, too. I guess a lot of us just needed some time out to consider our situation.

I decided to attend the School of Applied Theology in Berkeley, California. One of the better moves I have made.

Applied theology meant studying theology in view of putting it into practice in the everyday world. Theology as we had done it in the seminary was something we learned in our heads. In the Berkeley program, our teachers wanted us to be aware that theology is for people. We didn't just talk theories. We actually went out in the field. For our social science course, we went into a gym and slept on the floor with the homeless. We visited the soup kitchen in San Francisco and lined up outside with everybody else waiting for a meal. Then we went in and sat down with the regular clientele and ate and talked with them. We also visited and talked with prostitutes. One young lady I spoke with came from a terrible family background. Her father was an alcoholic and her mother a drug addict. Her father was often with other women, but her mom was so out of it that for the most part she didn't care. The mother prostituted herself to pay for her drugs. The daughter had not finished her eighth grade year. Without any education or skills, she had to turn to prostitution to survive. The purpose of encounters such as these was to help us get to know people who live at the margins of society – not from the outside, but from within, by "walking in their moccasins," so to speak. Such people are not fictional characters or statistics. They are God's own people in distress.

Sometimes those in desperate need are found right under our own roof. I am thinking of a brother Viatorian priest named Father Ed. While I was at Berkeley, I learned he was living in Oakland in a rehabilitation house sponsored by a former alcoholic judge who had used his money to help other alcoholics. I went to visit Father Ed and he told me his story. While he was still a priest in good standing, he had stolen the bishop's car. The police caught him, but the bishop did not want to press charges. Father Ed gradually worked his way to California where he got so low that he was literally eating out of garbage pails. One day, a kind gentleman discovered who he was and told him about a house just for priests in which they could live until they sobered up. I visited Father Ed in this house. Later, I learned that he got out and went to Phoenix, Arizona, where he found a job in a Catholic high school teaching French. He couldn't stay at it, unfortunately. He fell off the wagon and ended up on the streets again. I learned later that he had died. May he rest in peace.

Life moved at a different pace during my sabbatical year. I needed it. I lived in the Servite residence, not far from campus. For a small fee, I had room and board and use of the house, including the washing machine and dryer. The meals at the Servite house were fantastic, so I rarely felt the need to go out. Not being with a community of Viatorians, I socialized with my fellow students. There were about thirty of us in the class. Every Saturday and Sunday I would wander through the campus to watch the different goings on. Berkeley has been a colorful place ever since the hippie movement of the sixties. I particularly enjoyed the different musical groups. I remember that drums predominated – all kinds of drums from all kinds of cultures. I also played some golf with some retired Air Force priests. The golf clubs in San Francisco at this time let priests play for free. We only had to pay for the golf cart. The BART was not up and running in those days, but I found a ride sometimes with friends and made a few excursions into the waterfront of San Francisco.

One thing I made sure to do was keep in touch with Worldwide Marriage Encounter. During my sabbatical year, I made a "deeper weekend" in Seattle, Washington, and gave the first Marriage Encounter weekend in the city of Orange, California.

As my sabbatical year came to an end, I still didn't have a plan for my future. I did not apply for the degree program because I didn't think I needed it. All it would have meant was more work and another degree hanging on my wall. After studying applied theology, I wanted to get out there and start applying. I was never a big fan of school, anyway. What I needed was a call – a vocation – and that is exactly what I got.

Different Fields

Holy Cross Parish – Morgan City, Louisiana

One morning, I received a call from Father Dan Reardon, a Viatorian priest and pastor of Holy Cross Parish in Morgan City, Louisiana. He said that Father Larry Farrelly, one of the priests at Holy Cross, had been appointed the new vocations director for the Viatorians. Someone was needed to take his place in the parish. With the permission of the provincial, he was calling to ask if I might be interested. I was.

To tell the truth, I did not know anything about Morgan City. I didn't even know the place existed. Looking back, I would say now that I went because the call came at the right time and, as usual, I was answering a call for help. As it turned out, my time at Holy Cross was both wonderful and tragic. I was there in 1977 to see the creation of a new diocese, Houma-Thibodaux, of which Holy Cross was a member; I was also around when the tide of favor turned against the Viatorians.

My new assignment got off to an adventurous start. I drove all the way to Louisiana from Berkeley, stopping off in Las Vegas to visit old friends. I crossed some beautiful country in Arizona and had to make a pit stop in Phoenix because my tail pipe was dragging. During the long haul across the state of Texas, I stopped at the Alamo for a day and then continued on my way. As I approached Houston, I ran into some flooding that forced me to stop. I tried to find a room in a motel, but they were all sold out. Finally, I pulled over to a deserted gasoline station where I sat in my car for five hours waiting out the storm. I was pretty happy to get back on the road and find a motel where I could dry out for the night.

The rigors of the voyage did not turn out to be a forecast of my future in Morgan City. I spent three happy years as parochial vicar of Holy Cross. (Parochial vicar is a high sounding word for assistant pastor. Someone introduced it around this time and it became the "in" term to use for priests in a parish who assist the pastor.) In addition to Father Dan Reardon, I also worked with Viatorian Fathers Alan ("Al") Syslo and Joe Sanders. I got along with all the priests there – at least, I wasn't aware of any problems. Father Joe was a good looking, affable young man who liked people and wanted to be friends with them. Father Al was in charge of the liturgy and the decorations for the church. He did this task with a great deal of personal love and devotion. Father Dan was a short, overweight Irishman with light skin and a slowly receding reddish hairline over a ruddy complexion. He had a happy go lucky air about him and was always singing. He was a gentle, warm person who would do anything for you.

Life was exciting and rich at Holy Cross, a combination perhaps of southern hospitality and the feeling of renewal that followed the Second Vatican Council.

My colleagues were inventive in their liturgical celebrations and deeply in touch with their people. Father Al worked with the Acosta sisters, Peggy and Charlotte, to create beautiful and experiential liturgies. For my part, it took me some time to get used to the round altar in the church of Holy Cross. I like to see the people in front of me when I'm preaching.

Then there were the grand communal celebrations: Every Labor Day weekend, Bishop Warren Boudreaux would go out in a special boat into the middle of the Atchafalaya River and bless all the shrimp vessels as they passed by him. Of course, all the captains tried to out do each other by having their boats specially decorated for the occasion. It was a beautiful sight, all those shrimp boats circling the bishop's stationary boat. The blessing meant a great deal to the fishermen. The Gulf of Mexico is host to sudden storms, and not a few men are lost each year on the high seas. It's treacherous, hard work, and the fishermen are more than happy to have their boats blessed by God. The bishop knew this and was happy to be out there – though the sacrifice was apparent. Under the hot sun, he stood fully vested in a heavy chasuble and miter, holding on to his shepherd's staff with his left hand while he used his right hand to bless the boats with holy water. The perspiration just rolled off of him. All the priests of the diocese were with him, but only he could do the actual blessing. We were there for moral support . . . and to eat the mountains of shrimp that the Knights of Columbus cooked up in large brass kettles. What a feast!

Indeed, I have very happy memories of Louisiana cooking. Our cook at the rectory was Aline Reaux, an African-American lady who specialized in Cajun food. Her specialty was seafood gumbo soup. She did wonders with the shrimp and crawfish the parishioners would often drop by at the rectory. A casual atmosphere presided over the rectory – as casual, that is, as Grand Central Station! In my religious life, I had grown accustomed to the cloistered style of living in which lay people were not allowed to venture into the quarters of priests or sisters. At Holy Cross, people were always walking in and out like they owned the place.

The climate was mild, though sometimes quite humid. My allergies were in full swing, but at least I could sleep at night. The beauty of the area was undeniable. I remember taking long walks along the bayou and seeing the alligators swimming and sunning themselves. Never saw anything like that back in Southie! I profited from the slower pace of life to pick up my violin again; after all, I had promised Mother Prioress I would stay at it. I worked on some Irish jigs and reels but I didn't go public . . . yet. That was to come.

Daily Mass was in the evening at 5:30 P.M., so the mornings were somewhat easy going. At one of our house meetings we decided that each of us would take one weekend off a month, instead of one day off during the week. I decided to use my weekends to continue with my Marriage Encounter work. I dedicated myself to giving weekends in New Orleans, Lafayette, Baton Rouge, and the new diocese of Houma-Thibodaux, Louisiana. During my three years in Morgan City, I gave about thirty weekends. My first weekend in Houma-Thibodaux had about sixty couples in attendance. (The hotel was filled up the first night, so I had to share a room with the executive couple. They were a bit embarrassed, to say the least!) I was also asked to be team priest for the Marriage Encounter weekend in Bogotá, Colombia, South America. The United Nations Peace Corp couples living in Bogotá wanted a weekend – but in English. So, the team couple and I went and gave a powerful weekend there. Marriage Encounter was a perfect solution for what to do on my weekends. Instead of just wandering about, as it were, I went forth with a purpose. Not that I didn't enjoy working as a parish priest. I did, but I appreciated the added dimension of relationship with our team couples as well as the couples who were making the Marriage Encounter weekends.

In 1978, I managed to put together the book *Priesthood and Brotherhood – 1978 Directory of Vocations for Men*. It was published by Paulist Press, dedicated to my mother, and included a forward by Bishop Warren L. Boudreaux. *The Directory* contained a description of the spiritual goals, entrance requirements, types of apostolic works, and people to contact for the diocesan priesthood and religious orders in the United States. I can't mention this effort without also speaking of Nick and Alice LaRocca. Nick was Grand Knight of Knights of Columbus Council 12179 in Morgan City and the motivating force behind my desire to distribute *The Directory* throughout the country. Mr. Paul Vella, co-owner of the St. Mary Journal in Morgan City, was also very helpful to me in getting this book published.

I was very happy in Morgan City and could have stayed tucked away there for years. That was not to be, however. We Viatorians fell out of favor and the tide gradually changed.

At least at the beginning, there had been enthusiasm on both sides of the equation. The Viatorians had come to the New Orleans Archdiocese at the invitation of Archbishop

Philip M. Hannan, D.D. He had been looking for someone to take charge of the Morgan City Archdiocesan Holy Cross High School and Holy Cross Community Parish. It wasn't an easy slot to fill. Morgan City was sort of the Siberia of the archdiocese, way out in the western part of the territory. Father Mike Malley, C.S.V., mentioned to the archbishop that there were four Viatorians looking for a parish with a school attached. Seemed like a match made in heaven. Fathers Dan Reardon, Larry Farrelly, Joe Sanders and Al Syslo came down to Morgan City in 1974. I arrived in 1977 to replace Father Farrelly.

Unfortunately, some people down south are still fighting the Civil War. I hope this is not too shocking for lay people to read, but sadly priests also can be guilty of xenophobia: the hatred of outsiders. The priests of the New Orleans Archdiocese, and later the newly formed Diocese of Houma-Thibodaux, never really accepted us. A friend told me he heard that they did not like all of us northerners coming down there to take over the parish. Looking back, I think the real reason for the antagonism was that the priests of the Houma-Thibodaux area were jealous of our success in the parish. We were able to run things and still allow each priest to take a weekend off each month. We Viatorians were also innovative with our homilies. Sometimes this created a bit of controversy among more traditionally minded parishioners. In any case, Bishop Warren Boudreaux, the first bishop of the Diocese of Houma-Thibodaux, under pressure from his diocesan clergy, eventually gave in and decided to terminate our contract. When he came down to Holy Cross for the confirmation ceremony he told us that he wanted us to leave by June 1, 1979.

When the people who liked us heard the news they gathered together in the schoolyard and paraded around with posters and banners reading, "Keep the Viatorians!" "Don't let the Viatorians go!" "We love our Viatorian priests!" It was quite a sight to behold and even made the local news. This was a great sign of affirmation and we really appreciated it. Clearly, the majority of the parishioners loved us and wanted us, but the few who were against us were those with the greatest influence over the bishop.

And the end of the story? We all left the parish in June 1979 and returned to Chicago. Father Dan Reardon and I drove back in his car (along with his two huge German Shepherds). Father Dan took a sabbatical year. He is presently the priest in charge of the Villa Desiderata in McHenry, Illinois. Father Joe Sanders eventually left the priesthood to get married. Father Larry Farrelly, whom I replaced at Holy Cross, also left the priesthood. Father Al Syslo is now doing social work in California. For my part, I was assigned to St. Viator Parish in Chicago.

One activity from the Morgan City years that would figure into my future was my involvement in the Beginnings Experience movement for people suffering the painful loss of a spouse through divorce, separation, or death. Three ladies from Morgan City, Eva Dell Billiot, Mary Theriot, and Nina Macalusa went with me to Houston to make a Beginnings Experience weekend. In one of the activities during this weekend, the priest leader takes the individual through a special kind of experience to help him or her close the door to the past and live for the future. I was impressed with the weekend and eager to launch a Beginnings Experience in Morgan City. Unfortunately, I was unable to get my plan off the ground because of the Viatorian departure from Holy Cross. But the idea stayed with me – just on hold.

It was with a sigh of nostalgia that I left my three-year assignment at Holy Cross Parish in Morgan City. I had experienced southern hospitality first hand. I had enjoyed a special relationship with many people in the parish: Nick and Alice LaRocca who accepted me as part of their family; Dr. Frank and Katherine Distefano, and Cedric and Rowena La Fleur, who often invited me to be part of their prayer groups; Deacon Andrew Dragna who assisted us with the liturgy; Mamie Bergeron, principal of Holy Cross Elementary School and a good friend; and Agnes and Noah Solar who have kept in touch over the years – just to name a few. I missed all of my friends in the Holy Cross community and the life that we shared together in the parish.

And I missed the seafood gumbo, too.

St. Viator Parish – Chicago, Illinois

For the next three years, I was assistant pastor of St. Viator Church at the corner of Addison and Keeler, one of the oldest churches in the Archdiocese of Chicago. Father Tom Wise, C.S.V., was the pastor and the other assistants were Viatorian Fathers Don Lund and Tom Long. Father Ed Cardinal, C.S.V., retired, was in residence. The rectory was a huge three-story building with three long flights of stairs. When I first arrived, I had to live on the top floor in a small, poorly ventilated room. I sweat in summer and froze in winter. Eventually I was able to move to a more comfortable room on the second floor.

During this period, I was somewhat preoccupied by the need to resolve a serious hernia problem. The damage had been done one morning in Morgan City while I was running around the high school racetrack trying to keep fit. I felt a tug in my lower left side. The following medical exam revealed that I had a hernia necessitating immediate surgery. I had the operation, but it didn't stick; the hernia broke free again while I was carrying my traveling bag. After my transfer to St. Viator, I decided to have the surgery done again, this time in Chicago where I thought I could get the best doctor. My primary doctor wanted me to hold off for awhile, but the pain and discomfort were too much. I went under the knife again, and again the hernia broke, this time while I was in mid-swing on the golf course. The frustration I was feeling at this point cannot be imagined. People have told me that this procedure is in the category of minor surgeries, but I have to tell you that it was no fun any time I had it done.

Finally, my friend Father Tom Kinney told me about the Shouldice Clinic north of Toronto which specialized in hernia operations. Apparently, their new procedure had you in and out of the hospital in three days or so. I contacted the clinic and arranged for the surgery. Since it was a repeat surgery, however, I had to sign a release for the hospital to be willing to do the job. I didn't care. I was a desperate man. Knowing I would also need some help with the logistics in Toronto, I contacted Worldwide Marriage Encounter and found a couple in the area. They met me at the airport, drove me to the hospital, and after my week's hospitalization, took me into their home for a short while before I returned to Chicago. This was a beautiful example of how Worldwide Marriage Encounter is "family."

Two people stand out in my memory of the Shouldice Clinic: the doctor who did the surgery, because he did an excellent job, and the head nurse who made us grown men march up to her pill station every day at 11:00 A.M. where she distributed a pill to each of us with great pomp and ceremony. While the surgery was a great success, the stay in the clinic was not marked by great concern on the part of the staff. Rarely did the nurses come into our rooms. They wanted us to walk down to the nurses' station for all our needs. We even had to walk downstairs for our meals. They also stressed the need to use the stationary bicycles in the hallway. We had no televisions in our rooms; the nurses wanted us up and moving – no sitting around. It was like the repeating voice you hear at the airport on the moving sidewalk, "Keep moving. Keep walking." And when the doctor came in to remove my stitches, he had no mercy on me. "Don't be a cry baby," he said, as he gently but forcibly pulled out the steel stitches.

I let out a loud "ouch!" The patient in the other bed said nothing. He was next – and he had a double hernia. You could hear him a mile away. (For those of you out there facing this procedure, be reassured. They use paper stitches these days. Lucky!)

The story has a happy ending. After sixteen good years, I can confidently state that the Shouldice Clinic surgery was a success. Interestingly, I had another hernia operation done on my right side in 1993 by Dr. James Kane Sr., former physician for the Saint Viator High School athletic department. By this time the surgery had been greatly simplified. It was over in three hours; then I went home. What amazing advances we have made in medicine!

During my time there, the church building of St. Viator had its own tale of damage and repair thanks to a fire that swept through the lower level sanctuary. Everything had to be redone. I suggested that we put in moveable chairs, but Father Wise chose to restore the basement church to its original condition. On another occasion, a windstorm blew out the magnificent circular stained glass window above the choir loft. It was restored to its original splendor and a protective sheet of plastic secured it for the future. Whenever I said Mass on a clear day, I could see rays of different colors streaming though the rose-colored glass of the window into the church. It was breathtaking.

I gave a number of Marriage Encounter weekends during my three years at St. Viator's. I also put on a "Family Encounter Weekend" in the St. Viator cafeteria. We used the long tables in the cafeteria to make large "V shapes" that served as each family's home place. Whenever they finished the projects we assigned, they put them on the tables so that by the end of the weekend each home was fully "furnished." Presenting teams included adults and young people. We also worked in films and overhead projections. At the end of the weekend, we asked parents and their children to share with us what they had learned. I remember one father stood up and said that he had come to know his teenage daughter a little better; he was able to communicate with her and listen to what she was trying to say to him. I call that a minor miracle.

The Beginnings Experience work that I had begun in Morgan City was opened to me again in the Chicago area where the movement already existed. There were at this time two distinct movements, one for the divorced/separated and another for the widowed. Since I was still interested in working as a team priest for Beginnings Experience, I chose to concentrate on weekends for those who had lost a spouse in death. I met some wonderful people through Beginnings Experience. Mary Manton helped me with my talks. I also worked with Emelia Alberico who is now the former national executive for Beginnings Experience in the United

States. When the two groups merged, I stayed on as a team priest until I left Chicago in 1983.

I made some friends among the parishioners of St. Viator. Father Kinney and I did things together until he passed away. We would go to the movies on my day off. If he couldn't go with me, I would go alone. Actually, I dreaded my day off because I really did not know what to do with myself. Days off in Morgan City had been no problem. The weather was perfect and there were a lot of friends available for a round of golf. In Chicago, the inclement weather was sometimes a problem. I did have a membership with the Y.M.C.A., so I could go for a work out and then find a place to eat afterwards by myself. I always had my Worldwide Marriage Encounter contacts. Nonetheless, for the first time, I really knew loneliness

One of my special memories of St. Viator's grew out of a homily I gave one Sunday morning. I have been preaching for many years now and, I have to tell you, it sometimes gets boring. I guess the main reason is that no one ever bothers to stop afterwards to say whether they liked the homily or not. On one occasion, however, I got some incredible feedback. I decided to use my homily that Sunday to encourage parents to develop some kind of liturgical celebration in the home. I suggested that they bless each other every night, as well as their children before sending them off to bed. They could place their hands on each other's head and pray silently for awhile and then make the sign of the cross on the forehead while saying, "May God bless you and I bless you."

I enjoyed giving this homily. I felt that I was making some kind of an impression on my people. A kind of silence fell over them while I was talking. I thought, "Hey, I am saying something important and my people are really listening to me!" But, as usual, the members of my congregation passed me by after Mass without saying a word. I was a little depressed. I thought for sure I had struck pay dirt this time and someone would say something to me. Nothing. What can you do? I just let it go and went about my business.

A few weeks later, I received a letter from a woman who had attended that particular Sunday Mass. She was so happy to have been present and to have heard my homily. She wrote in her letter that she had done exactly what I described that very Sunday evening. She had gone into her baby's room and put her hands on the baby's head and made the sign of the cross while saying the words, "May God bless you and I bless you." To her dismay, the next morning when she went in to check on her baby, she found that the child had died sometime during the night. It was a classic case of "crib death." She was distraught by the death, but she was also thankful for having blessed her baby with her love the night before.

I still have that letter in my files. Every so often, when I feel blue, I take it out and read it again to give me a lift. I hope that all of you who read this little anecdote will be moved to initiate this daily spiritual ritual in your home.

After three years at St. Viator's, my provincial suggested that I take another sabbatical – maybe work towards another ministry. How did I feel about clinical pastoral education? I knew that I was not getting into the spirit of my rather conservative parish. Admittedly, I had been spoiled by my time in Morgan City. I couldn't shake the memory of the vibrant life I had known there: the rich, meaningful liturgies, the excitement of a rectory always full of people, the warmth of southern hospitality, not to mention the indulgence of my craving for crawfish étouffée and Cajun fried catfish . . . missing all this, I think I had gradually become depressed, though I didn't fully realize it. I definitely needed a change and was more than happy to accept my provincial's suggestion.

Hospital Chaplain

From 1982 to 1983, while living at our retirement residence, I picked up two credits for six months of study in the Clinical Pastoral Education Program at Lutheran General Hospital in Park Ridge, Illinois. The program was demanding but enriching. Each morning, my five classmates and I met for a brief period of prayer, followed by classes, and then visitations to patients in the hospital. We were responsible for keeping a record of our visits. Once a week, each of us presented to the class a typewritten report, called a "verbatim," of one of our visits. The verbatim summarized the dialogue – the questions and answers – which took place between us and a patient. We would listen to each other's verbatims and then give positive or negative criticism about how the interview had been conducted.

Each of us had to spend one night a week on call at the hospital for any emergencies that arrived. The ER nurse would let us know when we were needed. Our job was to be there for the friends and family of a patient, doing whatever we could for them until they left the hospital. In the event of a DOA (Dead on Arrival), we had to interview the immediate relatives and get a signature on the death certificate. This was sometimes a heart-rending experience. I remember the ER nurse waking me up one night to come assist with the family of a little girl who was DOA. The family was from the eastern part of the globe and, as was their custom, they were all there howling and crying over the death of the child. It broke my heart, but at the same time I had to get through the administrative stuff with them. I was happy when it all finally came to an end and I could get back to my room.

My initial plunge into hospital ministry was followed by more study the following spring. I spent three months attending the Clinical Pastoral Program at Alexian Brothers Hospital in Elgin, Illinois. I received a one credit C.P.E. certificate. The main object of these studies was to serve the patient better. Emphasis was on learning by experience. We also talked a lot about learning to get along with each other and the hospital staff. In addition to a weekly verbatim report, each student at Alexian Hospital had to prepare an interdenominational worship service on the hospital's closed circuit TV.

During this period, I also had the chance to realize a musical dream: I played in the second fiddle section of the Wright Junior College Orchestra. I doubted I had enough talent to play in the orchestra, but they accepted me and I found it to be a thrilling challenge. We were a real symphony orchestra with all the instruments you would expect to find. We played some pretty tough classical music, too. We practiced in the music department rehearsal room and gave our concerts in the large school auditorium. I did not like the regimentation of the orchestra leader, but I stayed with the orchestra for one year. I know that I am not a great violinist, but I was able to pull the bow back and forth with the other violinists – and a good number of times I was on the right notes. On one occasion, our section acted as the backup orchestra for a very talented solo violinist. It was a formal affair for which we all had to wear black jackets and ties. I was very proud to be playing with a real orchestra and even dragged two of my colleagues to a concert so they could witness the fact for themselves.

After I completed my year of C.P.E. training, an opening came up for a chaplain at the Sunrise Humana Hospital in Las Vegas. Since I had spent nine happy years in Las Vegas teaching at Bishop Gorman High School, I jumped at the chance to go back again. When the provincial asked me if I were interested, I said an emphatic and enthusiastic, "Yes!" I stayed there for three years, from 1983 to 1986.

Although I was officially attached to Sunrise Hospital, I was in residence at St. Anne's Catholic Church near Bishop Gorman High School. St. Anne's church is a blend of the contemporary and traditional; that is to say, it has air conditioning and a nice long aisle that is a real selling point for brides to be. The rectory is modern and comfortable. In addition to a private bath, my room also had a small living room. The parishioners were for the most part well to do families. Many of them lived in nice, one-family houses with a lot of grass on the lawn. It seemed like everyone had a pool, but that was probably just an indication of the prosperity of the times. People were coming to Las Vegas because of the low taxes and lovely weather.

I had a full schedule during this period. Usually I started the day by saying the 8:00 A.M. Mass in the church. I could expect to find the Di Martino boys, Ricky and Mark, with their dad in the congregation. I was a regular at their restaurant and we got pretty close. I came back to Las Vegas some years later to baptize Mark's first baby. After breakfast at the rectory, I left for the hospital around 9:30 A.M. I worked with two sisters at the hospital: Sister Lydia Wendl, F.S.P.A., and Sister Muriel Stork, F.S.P.A. We would take the computer printout of patient names and divide the list between us; then we would visit each Catholic patient. I usually took the intensive care floor since the patients there were the ones most likely to take a turn for the worse. I learned to anoint them and give them communion then and there so that I would not have to get out of bed in the middle of the night to anoint them later. The calls I came out for at night were usually accidents, births, or DOAs. I usually didn't mind these nocturnal visits. Las Vegas, unlike Chicago, does not really get bitter cold at night. It was, in fact, very comfortable, and the hospital was only a ten-minute drive.

Work in a hospital is continually in flux. People come and go and the situations are such that you couldn't come up with them in your wildest imagination. I have some interesting tales to tell, but the most dramatic I think is that of the "Dragon" lady. In order to understand this story, you have to know a little history about public transport in Las Vegas. The horse and buggy industry flourished along the strip. It was expensive, but it was very popular with honeymooners and vacationers. The taxi cab companies did not appreciate the competition.

One night I was called into the intensive care unit to find a Catholic woman in a coma. I anointed her and then spoke to her husband. They were both from Waterbury, Connecticut. Evidently, the lady was a former nun who was presently working as a schoolteacher. The couple had been married for two and a half years and were on their way to a belated honeymoon in Hawaii. They had wanted to stop in Las Vegas briefly just to say they had seen it and to try a little gambling. After checking into the hotel, they decided to take one of the buggy rides around town. It seemed like a nice, relaxed way to see the strip. They got into the buggy and things were going along nicely when suddenly the horse bolted across the sidewalk and into an empty lot along the strip. As the horse raced along, one of the wheels of the carriage hit a rock causing the driver and the Dragons to be thrown onto the ground. Upon landing, Mrs. Dragon struck her head and was immediately immobilized. Her husband suffered a few broken ribs while the driver walked away with some minor injuries. The ambulance that arrived took them all directly to Sunrise Hospital.

For about a week, I stopped in to see how Mrs. Dragon was doing. She remained in a coma. Her husband finally had to hire a special plane with the appropriate life support gear to take her home. It cost him a small fortune. Things did not improve for the Dragons. Within weeks of returning home, Mr. Dragon suffered a fatal heart attack while having lunch with some friends. He had just come from his wife's school were he had thanked the students for their prayers and cards following the accident. Because of the bad publicity that resulted from this awful tragedy, coupled with pressure from the taxicab companies, the city of Las Vegas cancelled the horse and buggy industry on the strip.

During my three-year stay at St. Anne's, I tried to get Worldwide Marriage Encounter moving in the Las Vegas area, but I did not have many couples who wanted to take over the executive position. Three executive couples quit within a five-month period. I was, in fact, an executive priest without an executive couple. I did give two weekends, one in Orange, California, and another in Phoenix, Arizona. As for Beginnings Experience, I was the only team priest in the Las Vegas area from 1983-1986.

Though my daily concern as chaplain of Sunrise Hospital was the illnesses of other people, I knew that I was entering into the twilight years of my own life. As usual, I had trouble with my allergies. Since my time in Rock Island, I had been receiving weekly allergy shots, one in each arm. My body had finally had enough. One day, I came back to the rectory after receiving my shots and suddenly felt very ill. I called for help. Father Jack McVeigh, the pastor at St. Anne's, heard me and rushed to my aid. He brought me back to the doctor who immediately took me in and gave me a shot of adrenaline. I think the doctor thought I was going to die on the table. He looked pretty shaken.

Maybe as a result of the shots, I started to suffer severe heart palpitations. On many occasions, I would wake up at night with a wild pounding in my chest. I thought I was having a heart attack. I would do some deep breathing and after what seemed like hours I would become so exhausted from this activity that I would fall back asleep, usually with my rosary in my hand. Every time I asked my primary doctor about it he told me not to eat two hours before going to bed. He believed I had a hiatal hernia and the food was backing up on me. Another time he told me that I should raise the head of my bed two or three inches to put my body on a slant. I obeyed his advice and it did seem to make a difference.

Between the hospital and my own declining health, I had a lot of material for meditation. For one thing, I began to realize how we are gradually prepared for death by the little deaths and resurrections we experience everyday. The word "death" for us usually means that final, one-way ticket home; but, in reality, we die to ourselves all the time. We also experience little resurrections. Sleep is a kind of death, but it also gives us new life. Illness will stop us in our tracks, but we also learn the life-giving properties of rest and recuperation. It's good for us to experience death and resurrection in little ways because it teaches us that we must die to ourselves in order to live. The individual psyche must give way to a better understanding of who we are, not isolated and alone, but vitally connected to others. I have seen couples come on Marriage Encounter weekends with the specific end of changing their spouse. No way. For a relationship to work, each partner has to decide to die to himself or herself and live for the other.

My time at St. Anne's had its sunny side. For one thing, I had plenty of other Viatorians living nearby to do things with during my off hours. Every Thursday morning around 6:30 A.M., Father Ed Anderson and Msgr. Ben Franzelli would meet me for a round of golf. Sometimes Father Elwood LaVoy would join us. At that time, the Desert Inn golf course allowed priests to play for free. We only had to pay for the carts. The weather was great and the price was right. We had a good thing going and I loved every minute of it. There were also many happy hours spent at the pool adjacent to St. Anne's. I remember the energizing feeling of the water evaporating quickly off my skin as I came out of the pool into the hot sun. After a round of golf or a dip in the pool, I could head back home to do some studying, write some letters or a sermon for the following Sunday, practice my violin or guitar, or just read. The days go by fast when you are enjoying life, and I was indeed.

At one point, I ventured to take a violin course at the University of Las Vegas. The teacher told me that I did not have the talent to play with the university orchestra. He suggested that I try out for another, less prestigious orchestra. His words kind of discouraged me, so I didn't follow through, though I did continue to practice.

While I was stationed in Las Vegas, my old friend Chester Balinski and his wife passed through on their way back from Hawaii. They were actually staying with another friend in Las Vegas, but we were able to get together for a few days. On the day they were heading home, I was shocked to receive a call from Chester that his wife had become sick on the plane before they took off and had passed away en route to the hospital. I couldn't believe it. I visited the hospital morgue and said a little prayer for her soul. Then Chet took her remains back to Boston for the funeral services.

During my years at St. Anne's, I used to invite my mother to come out and visit me. She had stayed very active over the years. She and my sister Terry took a trip to Florida together with a senior citizens group. She also went to Hawaii with a friend. For awhile she had problems with varicose veins, but following an operation and a painful recovery – during which she hardly complained – she was able to get on with life again. Mom made the trip to see me in Las Vegas a few times, though eventually it was too much for her. She was then in her late eighties and failing in health.

I loved my mother very much and wanted to be near her during the twilight years of her life. I started to keep an eye open for a position in the Boston area. In June 1985, I saw an ad in the *National Catholic Reporter* saying that Father Paul McLaughlin at Immaculate Conception Parish in Marlboro, Massachusetts, was looking for an assistant. Marlboro is about a forty-minute drive from South Boston. When I went back east for my vacation in August, I visited with Father McLaughlin. I fell in love with the church and the area. My brother Jim and his wife Jackie lived there, and it also held some nostalgia for me since the Viatorians from Canada had taught there for a few years. I let Father McLaughlin know that I was interested in the position. The interest was mutual.

When I returned to Las Vegas, I told Father McVeigh that I was returning back east to be close to my mother since she was getting along in years. My provincial gave the okay and it was a done deal. I sent most of my stuff to Marlboro by post and loaded the rest of it into my Chevy. After spending some time at the provincial house in Arlington Heights during the summer of 1986, I arrived in Marlboro in September.

Once upon a time I had strained at the bit to leave my family and realize my vocation to be a priest. Now, with thirty-four years of priesthood behind me, I was returning home to my mother. I guess my Heavenly Father wanted me to look after her one more time.

Full Circle

My mother lived for Monday night bingo at St. Augustine's hall in South Boston. The whole evening was steeped in ritual. She loved to go early and get her favorite seat. During the interlude that followed, Msgr. McDonnell, the pastor, would stroll by and they would flip a card from the deck, playing for the high stakes of twenty-five cents. My mother thought it was quite a feat when she managed to pull a higher card than her priest and pastor. She played bingo with a passion, and won a few times, though she was forever complaining that she had missed the big pot by one number.

Yes, mother loved to play bingo . . . but I hated it. I came down from Marlboro on Monday evenings and brought her to the bingo hall. After hanging around awhile to make sure she was settled, I would have dinner with Msgr. McDonnell and Father Joe Kane at St. Augustine's rectory. I would then return to my mother's apartment and later, between 9:30 and 10:00 P.M., drive back to the bingo hall to pick her up and bring her home. I would stay overnight and return to Marlboro after lunch the next day. This was my schedule for three years, altered only by the occasional round of golf on the way to South Boston during the summer.

My mother lived in a tiny senior citizen apartment in South Boston. She had a living room and a bedroom, plus the bath and kitchen. Tony Billie, a special friend and neighbor, visited her every night. They were good for each other. On my overnight visits, my mother would always give me her bed to sleep in and take the pull out bed in the living room for herself. That was the way she wanted it. Next morning, I would say Mass for her in the kitchen before lunch. On special occasions, I would say Mass in the activity room of her housing project. My mother enjoyed showing off her son the priest to all the people in the project.

Mom liked to visit her grown-up children, but never at her own initiative. I take after her in this: I'm not much for instigating social activities, either. I usually do my own thing unless someone asks me to go along with them. I won't refuse an invitation – hopefully it's something I like to do! Mom was much the same way, but in her case I know it flowed from her desire to practice the spiritual works of mercy. Jesus told us that whatever we do to the least of his brothers, we do it to Him. This was my mother's philosophy of life. She was a soul devoted to service and didn't think of doing for herself. She preferred to be available, always ready to say "yes" to whatever was asked of her. On the other hand, though she wouldn't just drop in, she appreciated being sought out and included in family activities. She loved to be surrounded by her sons and daughter and her many grandchildren and great-grandchildren. Besides being the center of attention, I think my mother relished the knowledge that she was responsible for all these lives.

For my part, I was very glad to be in the neighborhood again. I enjoyed having the chance to say Mass for Mom on her birthday and to have my family around me for my big days: my birthday on May 12 and my anniversary of ordination on October 1. As a matter of fact, for my forty-third anniversary, we had a huge party at the Immaculate Conception rectory. My pastor, Father McLaughlin, was a great host, playing the piano for a sing-along and making sure that everyone had a great time.

My initial feelings about Immaculate Conception parish proved to be accurate. The people were fantastic and the office staff was like family. I loved serving there. I made a lot of good friends in the parish. One friend in particular was Eleanor Capolla of 35 Highland Street. Eleanor, a heavy set woman, suffered from asthma and had to be at home on oxygen twenty-four hours a day. I would make a communion call to Eleanor's once a week. We would pray together and I would give her the sacrament of the sick. She had a pleasant, friendly personality and we would spend some time talking during my visit.

Of course, I also got involved with Worldwide Marriage Encounter in the Boston area. I served as executive priest with Joe and Debby Deneen from 1988 to 1989. Father Bob McDonald, S.M., executive priest for the Maine Marriage Encounter Community, was also a good friend. During my first year, the New Hampshire Marriage Encounter Community asked me to be the presenting priest at one of their weekends. The scheduled team priest fell sick and I was called to take his place. I was received royally by the couples in New Hampshire, especially by Peter and Virginia Catelli. The weekend was a great success and since then we have stayed in touch. I saw them again in 1995 in Chicago when they attended a "Deeper Weekend" reserved for couples and priests on executive teams.

I had been looking forward to living near my family again, but sadness was not long to follow my arrival in

Marlboro. On March 25, 1986, my brother Al died after a painful battle with cancer. He lived his final days at home where his wife and children took care of him. I used to go and visit him regularly. People from the nearby hospice center came often, too. I really missed Al, particularly after I moved back to South Boston to look after Mom. I would have really enjoyed the chance to be closer to him. He was my favorite brother and always made my visits home something special. I would say that with Chester Balinski and Deacon Ed Gallagher, Al was one of my best friends in life.

Al's death was also very hard for my mother. She had been very close to Al and his family, often spending Christmas with them at their house in Wakefield, Massachusetts. My niece, Sandy Brooks, wrote this touching account of "Grammy" at Christmas time:

> Grammy spent a lot of Christmases with us in Wakefield. I'm not sure exactly when she started coming, but I must have been relatively little because I remember her always being there – which also prompted visits from Uncle Paul and Aunt Ginny and the kids, as well as Uncle Richie and Aunt Rita and the kids. Sometimes Uncle Vinny and Aunt Ginny. But Grammy loved to watch us open our presents and then she spent all day putting stuff together and playing lots of games. She taught me a lot about life in relating her stories as a young woman in Boston and raising all of her kids basically without help from Grandpa, whom I never met but wish I had . . . I never saw pictures of Grandpa because Grammy used to say, "He was a good man, but time took its toll." She and Dad also encouraged Greg, Beth, Bub and me never to drink . . . Grammy also taught me how to

crochet when I was in third grade. I still crochet to this day. Right now I am making blankets for Children's Hospital in Boston, to be distributed to the sick children. I'm sure Grammy would be working away making some as well if she were alive. I miss her terribly . . . She is constantly in my prayers.

After about three years in Marlboro, I noticed my mother was really starting to slow down. Even a forty-minute drive was too far away. I needed to get closer. As if Providence had already arranged everything for us, I found out that Sts. Peter and Paul, the parish in which I grew up, was in need of an assistant pastor. I applied for the position and got it. I served there from 1989 to 1992.

The parishioners and staff at Immaculate Conception gave me a big send off. Eleanor Coppola wrote a poem for me and read it at the celebration as a going away present. A local paper ran an article about my departure with the opening words, "He has pledged his life to the Father, but he's going home to mother." On the receiving end, South Boston's community newspaper heralded my return to Southie with a front-page picture and a headline reading, "Fr. Tom McCarthy Returns to His Home Parish." Under the article were the words, "Welcome home, Fr. Tom!"

There is a song called *Southie is My Home Town* which talks about people born on "A" Street, brought up on "B" Street, etc. I guess I had come full circle.

I can't say I minded going back to Southie. Even beyond the personal history that binds me to the place, I love the atmosphere of South Boston. Granted, it has changed a lot since the days I was playing "kick the bar" with my buddies in whatever vacant lot we could find. A kind of cultural revolution has taken place. The old tenement houses that I knew have been bought up and converted into condominiums, and a fresh, upwardly mobile feeling rests over neighborhoods that once lay in dire poverty. Some things never change, though, like the presence of the bay always over your shoulder and the fruits of the sea served up in Southie's many restaurants. My favorite walk is along Castle Island which juts out into Boston Harbor. It feels so good to breathe in that wonderful salt air. Truly, there's no place like home.

Things had changed quite a bit at Sts. Peter and Paul since my childhood. Originally, the parish consisted of a large Irish population. It also included a Lithuanian church (my brother Charlie and wife Ann were married there), St. Vincent de Paul Church, and Our Lady of Good Voyage waterfront chapel on the harbor across from the Pier Four Restaurant. This chapel had been built to take care of visiting Catholic sailors who came to the port of Boston.

When I was serving my country plugging away in the shipyards, most of the Sts. Peter and Paul's parishioners came from the federal housing that had been built for workers similarly engaged in the war effort. Afterwards, these buildings were converted into low-income housing and the demographics changed radically. By the time I returned, only about a hundred people attended Sts. Peter and Paul on a Sunday, a third of them youngsters. The collections were inadequate to pay for the maintenance and upkeep of parish property. Monday night bingo in the basement of St. Vincent de Paul's kept enough in the till to keep the parish running, but eventually the bishop and the parishioners together realized that something drastic had to be done. The church of Sts. Peter and Paul was closed in 1995. In January 1998, the rectory followed and the entire parish thereafter took the name of St. Vincent de Paul. The church and rectory were finally sold in October 2000 to a private developer who will build residential and affordable housing where they now stand. With the parish more consolidated, there are plans to buy a new rectory and build a new parish center across the street from St. Vincent de Paul Church.

Father Dave Murphy was the pastor of Sts. Peter and Paul when I arrived in 1989. Less than a year after my arrival, Father John Dooher took his place. Father John is a man of many talents: painter, guitarist, flutist, but principally singer. He has some interesting tales to tell. He had been one of the "singing priests" who raised money for the diocese by performing in parishes. Whenever Cardinal Cushing, the former Archbishop of Boston, was doing fundraising at Blinstrub's Restaurant in Southie (now closed), the singing priests were at his side.

Father John was a great inspiration for my own musical interests. I began to practice in earnest. My last year at Sts. Peter and Paul, Father John arranged that I should play the violin while he played the guitar and sang some Christmas carols before the Midnight Mass. It was beautiful. I played like I knew what I was doing. The people really enjoyed the concert. The following St. Patrick's Day, I entertained the crowd who came to watch the parade from our rectory. I played a few jigs and hornpipes. Everyone was pleasantly surprised that I was able to play some fast Irish traditional tunes. (Living in the rectory was a definite advantage on St. Patrick's Day – "Evacuation Day" for South Bostonians. The famous St. Patrick's Day parade would assemble at the Gillette Factory and then pass by our rectory at 55 West Broadway. It was a pleasure to be a spectator from the comfort of our rectory window since the parade goes on rain, snow, or shine. Local politicians never mind the exposure – especially around election time.)

Of course, the best part of being at Sts. Peter and Paul was the ease with which I could look after Mom. My sister Terry and I often took her out to her favorite restaurant, The Cock and Bull, once the hangout for the famous Gustin Gang of South Boston. Mom always enjoyed her order of baby lamb chops, complaining nonetheless that the carrots were never cooked enough. Over time, however, I watched her lose interest in going out. She became more and more feeble. I knew she dreaded going into a nursing home. In God's goodness, she never saw the inside of one. Furthermore, she remained active right up to the end. I have a photo of her taking a whirl as a passenger on her grandson Jim's motorcycle – in her seventies!

One day, Tony Billie called to let me know something was wrong. I immediately went to my mother's apartment and from there called for an ambulance. She was taken to Boston University Hospital. I followed in my car and was able to stay with her in the receiving room. Mom had suffered a stroke. She lingered on for about two weeks, most of the time in a coma, until she finally expired. At one point, she developed pneumonia. The doctor in charge met with the family. He suggested that although the pneumonia could be treated with medication, considering her advanced age and condition, it might be best to simply keep her sedated and out of pain until she breathed her last. We all agreed. Mom died at 12:55 A.M., October 18, 1989. She was ninety-two years of age.

Rose McKernan McCarthy had a grand funeral. The wake was held at Casper Funeral Home and the Funeral Mass at St. Augustine's parish church. At least six priests were present, including her eldest son who served as the main celebrant. I was too emotional to give the homily, so

Msgr. Tom McDonnell, the pastor of St. Augustine's, gave it for me. After communion, I was able to say a few words:

> Mother, I will miss you. You have been not only a mother to me, you have been a pal, a great friend, and a good companion. All of us gathered here today will miss you. Mother, I love you. All of us gathered here this morning love you. That is why we are here. Mother, in the name of your sons and their spouses and your only living daughter and all your grandchildren, great-grandchildren, and your great-great grandchildren, and all your relatives and friends assembled here this day, I want to ask the Lord God to give you everlasting peace and joy and happiness in that land beyond the sky. May your soul and all the souls of the faithful departed through the mercy of God rest in peace. Amen

The whole family was present, of course. And, God bless them, my senior citizen friends from Immaculate Conception Church in Marlboro, where I spent three years before coming to Sts. Peter and Paul Church, all came in a bus, first to the Mass, and then to Fairview Cemetery where we buried my mother. She was laid to rest directly over the grave of my father who had been buried there in February 1975.

As I write this, I can tell you that my mother's life has born fruit in twenty-eight grandchildren, fifty great-grandchildren, and five great-great-grand children. Nothing made her happier than to have all her children around her. She was proud of us all, and had good reason to be. From humble beginnings, we McCarthys had done pretty well for ourselves over the years.

My brother Jim retired from the army as a lieutenant. One of my favorite family photos shows my mother pointing to the Purple Heart that Jim received on the White House lawn in Washington, D.C. Jim was an engineer by profession. He was widowed twice and had one boy and two daughters. I have fond memories of both his wives, Dot and Jackie. Vincent worked in construction, specializing in air conditioning. He married Virginia (who passed away in 2001). Francis met his wife Rose while he was serving as a career man in the navy. They have three boys and one girl and live in Norfolk, Virginia. Charlie spent most of his life as a member of the Massachusetts National Guard. He also worked as a supervisor for a building and wrecking company in Boston. His logo, "the wrecker," is proudly displayed on his automobile license plate. He and his wife Ann had a boy and a girl and also raised an adopted daughter. Alfred, whom we lost in 1986, married June McCarthy. They had two boys, the youngest of whom died tragically as a young man in 1993. They also had two daughters. Al spent most of his life as an accountant. In his spare time he loved to sing and dance. He and his daughter Sandy were a popular square dance calling team that traveled up and down the eastern seaboard performing. Terry, my only living sister, married twice and had one girl and three boys. She worked most of her life as a secretary/accountant for the J.B. McCabe Construction Company in South Boston. She is now retired and living in New Hampshire. Paul retired from the Boston City Fire Department as a fire chief. He and his wife Ginny have three girls and two boys. Richard, the youngest of the family, served a number of years in the Army Reserves in Massachusetts. He lives in Quincy, Massachusetts with his wife Rita. They have two boys and three girls.

I think that Mom's death was particularly hard on my sister Terry, the only other woman in our family. They had been very close. Terry wrote me once how she remembered coming home from St. Augustine's school to find Mom at work ironing and listening to the soap operas on the radio. Every Saturday night they would head out to a show together. After Mom sold the house on Gates Street, she lived on the first floor of Terry's home on Broadway for awhile before moving into the project. Terry and her husband frequently went over to the hall to have lunch with her. The memory of their times together has stayed fresh in my sister's heart. As she wrote in a letter last May, "Mom was always there when you needed her – I sure miss her very much . . . it seemed that I was always with her."

After Mom died, I continued at Sts. Peter and Paul rectory because the Viatorians did not have any place to assign me. I kept busy. I attended courses at the University of Massachusetts downtown campus and in June 1991 received an Advanced Certificate Degree in Gerontological Social Policy at the John F. Kennedy Library in Boston. The purpose of this course was to help people realize that intergenerational programming may be the best way to serve the needs of the elderly and the young in our country.

I was unsuccessful in getting Beginnings Experience going in the Boston area; however, I found another way to help couples in the Retrouvaille Movement for troubled marriages. In 1990, along with Franciscan Fathers Fergus Healey and Claude Lenehan from the famous Franciscan Shrine on Arch Street in Downtown Boston, I helped launch the Retrouvaille Movement for the six states of New England. We cooperated with Ted and Iris Bjorn, former international coordinating team couple, and Warren and Brenda Chamberlain, former international secretary team. I found that Retrouvaille weekends were emotionally draining. It would take me several days to get my feet back on the ground again. After Father Jim Elliot, an Augustinian priest working in Retrouvaille, had a heart attack, I was the only Retrouvaille priest available for awhile. I was very happy when Father Fergus and Father Claude joined me. Father Fergus is presently the executive priest for the Retrouvaille movement in the Boston area.

During my time at Sts. Peter and Paul, I really felt my body slowing down. I had surgery on a bunion. Six months later I was still in pain. I was living at that time on the fourth floor of Sts. Peter and Paul rectory, affectionately called "Odd Fellows Hall" because it had so many priests living there. After the operation, I had to walk up the four flights of stairs backwards, one step at a time. Then I devised a pulley so the cook could send my meals up to me. More seriously, my heart palpitations grew worse. After a trip to the emergency room at St. Elizabeth's Hospital in Boston, I was recommended to a cardiologist. At first he thought that I had what is called a "lazy" heart, that is, beating under sixty. The possibility of a pacemaker came up, but in the end he was able to regulate things with medication. I was very grateful to God.

Yes, I was really facing my mortality. My journal from this period reads:

> I am feeling blue today, like the sky out there, for I am thinking about the finality of my life. My atrial frib is causing me to take stock of my future. My life depends, like so many of my senior friends, on 900 mgs of Rythmol, one Lanoxin, and one aspirin that I have to take daily. If they work, okay. If not, then I have to go through the scary procedure of getting an

electrical shock and have an illuminated microscope shoved down my throat to see if I have a blood clot in my heart. Your whole life takes on a new perspective when you realize that you are threatened by these unusual events that come from getting old. Scary. Scary. Scary.

In the summer of 1992, I received a letter from Father Patrick Render, the then provincial of the Clerics of St. Viator, asking me to be the director of the retirement residence in Arlington Heights, Illinois. I decided to accept this offer. I did not have any security in the Boston area because I was not ordained a priest for the Boston Archdiocese. Although I had been born in Boston and grew up there, my rightful place was with my religious family, the Viatorians. That was where I wanted to be. I also knew that I would be able to continue giving Marriage Encounter, Retrouvaille, and Beginnings Experience weekends in the Chicago area. As far as I could make out, this was God's will for me. I accepted to live out the rest of my life in this way.

Father John Dooher gave me a tremendous going away party at St. Vincent de Paul's church hall. All my family and friends were there to send me off. Father Dick Cannon, the present pastor of St. Vincent De Paul, has generously kept a place for me to stay on my occasional trips back to Boston.

The opportunity to direct the retirement center seemed to come at just the right time. I hadn't officially retired, but I knew that the position of director at the retirement center would provide a nice way of making the transition. From here on out, I thought, things are going to get much quieter.

Part III
Apostle for the Eucharist
(1996-present)

A Priest Forever

Retirement

Retirement isn't so bad, if you like bowling and golf.

Admittedly, it's an easy life to slide into, especially when you are surrounded by comfort. Take my situation, for example. The retirement center where I am living is long and carpeted throughout. A wooden rail runs along the wall for those who need help walking. The cathedral ceiling with high west-facing windows provides us with lots of light. Each of the sixteen rooms in the building is actually a suite including a bedroom, living room, and bath. We have air conditioning in the summer and individual thermometers to regulate the heat in winter. We all have our own TV sets. I have a radio bequeathed to me by the last tenant of my room. I even have a second hand computer. We all have our own automobiles and some of us have garages that open automatically – much appreciated on cold winter days. It is, in a word, sumptuous.

In addition to the physical amenities, a group of eight sisters with the Missionary Sisters of the Sacred Heart and Our Lady of Guadalupe from Mexico City take care of our every need. They cook our meals three times a day, clean our rooms, wash our clothes, and generally make us comfortable. We are treated like kings. We owe this high life to the hard work of our Viatorians in the field who support the community.

I was pretty lucky. Unlike some men who go overnight from fulltime work to doing nothing at all, I was eased into retirement. In fact, I never officially retired. I kind of slid into it. I was seventy-two years old – already way past legal retirement age – when my provincial asked me to be coordinator of the retirement center. I understood that this position was just a stepping stone to full retirement.

As coordinator, I was responsible for our elderly priests. It was my job to solve whatever problems stood in the way of their enjoying their well-earned retirement. The residents of the retirement center were in various stages of illness. I was on call day and night. I had to check on them often, get them to the doctor, dentist, podiatrist or pharmacy – sometimes the hospital or emergency room, as need be. If you have ever gone to the emergency room at your local hospital, you know what the experience entails: the entrance forms to be filled out, the endless hours waiting for the patient to be seen by the doctor, the x-rays and/or any other tests ordered, and finally, the wait for the doctor to declare whether the patient should stay overnight or go home. Then, if a stay is required, there's the follow up visit with a traveling bag of personal items.

Sad to say, but I date my memories of this period by recalling the Viatorians I helped lay to rest.

In my first year as coordinator, Father "Bip" Shiels died in his sleep one night. He was a good friend from my Las Vegas days. We also did some traveling around Arlington

Heights together. Letting him go was like saying goodbye to a big piece of my own life.

The following year, 1993, Father Mike Malley's earthly life came to an unexpected end. He had just been appointed pastor of St. George Catholic Church in St. George, Illinois, after being chaplain of Elmhurst Hospital. He looked forward with enthusiasm to this new position and began to take a great deal of interest in the job, even buying a computer to help him with the work. I helped him move into his new place and then heard a week later that he had had a heart attack. The doctor ordered immediate bypass surgery. Mike had a rough time recuperating. His heavy smoking did not help his recovery one bit. I went back and forth to Elmhurst hospital for about a year tending to Mike. Then he went to the re-hab center at the Alexian Brothers place. He finally came back home to the retirement center in Arlington Heights but lasted only about a year. The wake and funeral at St. Alexis's Church near Elmhurst were crowded with people, including a good number of priests and two bishops. I missed Father Mike a lot. He was family.

Father Manny Loughran also died in 1993. I witnessed his final breath in St. Joe's Nursing Home.

Two months later, Father Jerry Leahy died; he was followed by Father Frank Powers in 1995. Father Frank had come to the retirement center to recuperate. He only lived about seven months or so after joining us. He had to use a wheelchair and was on oxygen all the time; then, in the midst of all his sufferings, he developed prostrate trouble and the doctor suggested surgery. That was the end of him. He died in the hospital. The wake and funeral were held in our chapel at the retirement center.

As you can imagine, death began to figure into my thinking like never before. Even though I had my share of ailments, I had never really thought about dying. I was too busy living. Now, as director of the retirement home, death and I were getting acquainted.

I learned how men die. For example, Father Phil Clifford had been struggling with a fibrillating heart – just like me – when things suddenly took a turn for the worse. The first thing that struck me was when he had to give up the keys to his car. He cherished that car. It was his logo and prized possession. Then one day he offered me his Magnavox compact disc player. He loved the great composers and had about a hundred classical CD's. I knew the end couldn't be far off. And so it was. He had another attack and died in the hospital.

I began to wonder what my own ticket home was going to be like.

On the positive side, I learned that it's important to keep things in order and to prepare for that great day of homecoming. As a Catholic, I believe in the hereafter and that the Lord has a place waiting for me in heaven. At the same time, I'm not in too much of a hurry to get there because I have so many things I want to do before I leave this earth. I want to make my mark on the world by helping others know and live in the Lord. So many people are living to pile up a mountain of money. For what? Leaving behind us a legacy of faith and good works is the only thing that really matters.

In 1994, Father George Auger was appointed to replace me as coordinator at the center. Relieved of my primary caretaker responsibilities, I settled into life as a retired priest in the mold of the men I had just spent two years looking after.

I could feel age creeping over me. I didn't have the same energy any more. My heart had begun giving me problems again shortly after I arrived at the retirement center. My teeth hurt from nerve exposure on the upper right side, and the false teeth I got came to late to really help the situation. I should have taken care of it sooner. I started taking Ocuvite for macular degeneration. My left thumb was aching at the main knuckle, and I started doing exercise to relieve the arthritis in the right side of my back.

Worse than the physical degeneration, I had the elderly blues. You tell yourself that you deserve retirement. But deep down, you know you have been put out to pasture. Society doesn't expect anything out of you anymore; what's worse, you expect less and less from yourself. After all, what have you got to give? Haven't you seen your best years already? Now, it's just a waiting game, maybe long, maybe short, for your final exit. And then there is the loneliness that sets in. I had become pretty independent in my life and not too successful at cultivating relationships with my brother Viatorians. In a residence center of equally independent characters, I often felt isolated and alone.

To be fair, I did try to find ways to stay active. For example, I learned that two local nursing homes needed chaplains once a week. With the willingness of some of my confreres in the retirement center, we agreed to take turns saying the 4:30 P.M. Mass on Saturdays at the Lutheran Home, as well as the Sunday 2:00 P.M. Mass at the Church Creek Nursing Home. We still have four men going there on a rotation basis. In addition, fellow retiree Father Charles Maranto agreed to fill in on the chaplain's day off once a week at the St. Joseph Nursing Home operated by the Little Sisters of the Poor in Palatine, Illinois. I take the 11:00 A.M. Wednesday Mass there whenever Father Charlie can't go.

I owe a lot to Father Charlie for getting me out of the house from time to time. Once in awhile we do a round of golf together. If it weren't for Charlie, I would just go to the range and hit some golf balls by myself. I've never been one to initiate activities.

Charlie also got me involved with the senior citizens' bowling league at Beverly Bowling Lanes. I was introduced to a great group of people, all in their upper sixties and seventies and even eighties. Don't let the ages fool you; some of these bowlers are to be reckoned with. One Monday, for example, our team – in last place – had to face eighty-seven year old Fran Booth of the second place team. Her final score was higher than the four of us put together! (O.k., we were having an off night . . .) Actually, I haven't done too badly as a bowler. In the 1993 and 1994 Intergenerational Bowling Festivals held at Beverly Bowling Lanes, I was the highest scoring male senior bowler. I even got a write up in *Southie News*, my old hometown's newspaper. The festival was begun in 1992 by the District 214 Community Education fitness-festival-wellness program to encourage high school students to become better acquainted with senior citizens through a month-long bowling competition.

With more time on my hands, I decided to brush up on my violin playing. I began practicing some of the Irish traditional tunes; then, I heard about a traditional Irish music jam session being held every Wednesday night from 7:30 to 10:00 P.M. at the Irish Heritage Center in North Chicago. I finally mustered up enough courage to grab my fiddle and head down there. I discovered about ten or so musicians in attendance. Some played the tin whistle, others the accordion. One gentleman played the flute, another the guitar with a mouth organ attached to his head so that he could play it while strumming. One night a man who played the bag pipes came in, and then another who played the Irish drum. Musicians take turns playing while the others follow along. When it was my turn, I played the two songs that I had practiced and knew fairly well. I needed the music in front of me, but I got such a surge of confidence from playing with this group that I practiced like crazy and finally could play four songs from memory. I had reached another pinnacle in my life.

I managed to keep abreast of the modern world, too. I received a computer from some friends in Worldwide Marriage Encounter. I've taken some courses, but I really only use it for word processing and email. I also attended some classes on mind and body at Good Shepherd Hospital in Barrington, Illinois.

And so it went. Life as a retiree.

Now, you might say, "Hey, that's a pretty full life. Nothing to complain about." I suppose that would be correct except for one thing. I'm a Catholic priest. You don't stop being a priest because you've reached the golden age of sixty-five. Bowling, golf, and an occasional substitution at a nursing home aren't enough when you know deep down what you are, what you have, and what you can do. Is a priest like a plumber or a policeman that he just stops doing what he does one day? Do you put your Roman collar on a shelf next to your breviary and Mass kit and think, "Well, I won't be needing these anymore." Is that what happens? Certainly not. We priests are not businessmen or tradesmen or construction workers. We don't just stop going to work one day. What we are is marked on our souls for all eternity. "You are a priest forever, in the order of Melchizedek." (Ps 110:4; Hb 5:5-6, 6:20, 7:24)

I'll admit that I wasn't any different from most "retired priests." I accepted the primrose path to oblivion without any objections. My society told me my "usefulness" was past and I should just enjoy myself. So, that's what I did. That's what I would have kept doing if God hadn't grabbed me by the bootstraps. I guess I can say that, even at seventy-six years old, I still had a Heavenly Father who was looking out for me. He knew what was good for me and what wasn't. He wasn't about to stand by and watch me fade away into the horizon. We still had some big things to do together, my Father and I.

Audrey Santo

While I was stationed in the Boston area, I enjoyed an occasional get together with my brother Vincent and his wife Ginny. Sometime in 1990, a friend in their prayer group told them about little Audrey Santo and the oil bleeding from sacred images in her home.[7] Curiosity got the better of them and they drove to Worcester to see for themselves. They were so enthralled with what they found that they became regular pilgrims to the "shrine of a silent soul." They were also anxious to share their discovery with someone in the family. After their attempts to interest my other brothers failed, they started on me. Whenever we met for dinner, they were sure to bring up the subject of taking me along with them for a Wednesday Mass at the Santo home.

I wasn't too warm to the idea. For one thing, mystical phenomena were not my bag. For another, Vincent and

---

[7] For the whole story on little Audrey, see Thomas W. Petrisko, *In God's Hands: The Miraculous Story of Little Audrey Santo* (McKees Rock, PA: St. Andrew's Productions, 1997). Bishop Daniel P. Reilly's letter concerning Audrey Santo, as well as the first investigative report, can be found at the Diocese of Worcester web site: http://www.worcesterdiocese.org. Further information is available from Ray Delisle at Rdelisle@worcesterdiocese.org.

Ginny had just recently joined the prayer group and were displaying the usual evangelical tendencies of the newly converted. I didn't want to be lassoed. Their persistence, however, wore me out. Besides, they used a persuasive argument: "You are a priest and you should see for yourself." Fair enough. What did I have to lose?

From what Vincent and Ginny had told me, I had a pretty good idea of what was happening around Audrey Santo even before I crossed her threshold for the first time. In the beginning, the remarkable signs and wonders surrounding this little girl were known only to her family and a few intimate friends. Little by little, however, the word got out. People began stopping in to see Audrey and ask for her prayers. Individual visits grew into organized pilgrimages. Audrey finally succeeded in attracting media attention. She has been featured in the *Boston Herald*, the *Washington Post*, and *People Magazine*, and has been the focus of special reports on *20/20*, *Unsolved Mysteries*, and Boston's local TV magazine *Chronicles*. At twenty years of age now, Audrey Santo continues to astound those around her, defy scientific explanation, and rekindle the faith of hundreds who have visited her home in Worcester, Massachusetts. She is one of the marvels of our age.

History of a Silent Soul

Audrey Santo was born on December 19, 1983, the fourth child of Linda and Steve Santo. From the very beginning, Audrey was challenged by illness. She was born with breathing disorders and a heart condition that necessitated a twenty-four hour heart monitor. Notwithstanding the physical challenges, Audrey Santo was an intelligent, even precocious, little girl who demonstrated a passion for life. Her family remembers her as a bubbly, self-confident little one who liked to joke and tease. She was always the first member of the family out of bed in the morning, serving as the house alarm clock as she went from room to room. She learned to read before the age of four and had no qualms about being the center of attention. She loved to sing, tell stories, go out to eat, and watch her favorite videos. In short, she was a very normal little girl.

Many who knew little Audrey before the accident have commented that she radiated a beauty and purity exceptional for a child. She was a tiny twenty-three pounds at the age of four, but her soul gleamed out of her blue-green eyes. Her beautiful auburn brown hair is still lovingly tended by those who care for her. Even more than her physical endowments, little Audrey's spirit drew people to her. They wanted to pick her up and hold her. She seemed to exude love. When it came to religion, she revealed an early maturity in her relationship with God. They were already close friends. She told her mother that she didn't much like formal prayers. She just liked "to talk to God."

On the morning of August 9, 1987, four-year old Audrey was playing in the front yard with her brother Stephen. When Stephen went into the house, Audrey wandered into the backyard and somehow ended up face down in the four-foot deep pool. No one can say exactly how long she had been there when the family discovered what had happened. Paramedics were quick to arrive, but by then Audrey had no pulse and her eyes were fixed and dilated. What then ensued would become a pattern in Audrey's story: medical interventions, some grievously in error, always with the pessimistic predictions of doctors and the unquenchable hope of her mother and family.

Escorted by a police cruiser, the ambulance rushed Audrey to Worcester City Hospital. During the trip, her heart went into near cardiac arrest and the paramedics desperately administered Epinephrine and Atropine to stimulate its weakened beating. They may have given too large a dose for such a little girl. Upon arrival at the hospital, Audrey's heart had stopped completely. Shock treatment restored her pulse and her condition stabilized. She was transferred to University of Massachusetts Hospital where a series of questionable drug therapies may ultimately have resulted in more damage.

The doctors at UMH held out no hope for Audrey. They informed the family that she had sustained serious injury to her heart, lungs, and brain and that death was inevitable. But Audrey hung on. Days turned into weeks, and then weeks into months. Audrey could not communicate, but her eyes were open. Her brain was still governing all her bodily functions except for her breathing. She was diagnosed with Akinetic Mutism, a rare condition in which the patient is not quite in a coma but not able to speak or move, either.

After four months, it was time to move Audrey out of the hospital. Against the advice of medical personnel, Linda Santo decided her little girl should be cared for at home. She had good reason to want to care for her daughter herself: physical therapists had already broken both Audrey's legs at the knees, fracturing her tibias, and dislocated her right shoulder. For Linda, the only good care would be a mother's care. She sold her home and purchased a new, ranch-style house on South Flagg Street in Worcester. Family and friends helped juice up the electrical power needed to run the respirator, monitors, and other medical apparatus.

A Meeting at Medjugorje

Soon after hearing about the apparitions in Medjugorje, Linda had a strange dream one night that she interpreted to mean Audrey had to go to Medjugorje.[8] She called Father Pervan at St. James Church where the apparitions were happening and received an open invitation to come and be present with Audrey. A Yugoslavian airliner carried Linda, Audrey, and Audrey's nurse, Joyce O'Neill, nonstop from JFK in New York to Dubrovnik, Yugoslavia, on July 29, 1988. Linda had to buy six seats on the plane to accommodate her daughter's bed and equipment.

Two days later, on a Sunday night, Linda, Joyce, and Audrey were in the choir loft of St. James Church for an apparition. Father Slavko Barbaric arrived with the visionary Ivan Dragicevic. Audrey, a bit restless, was placed on the floor in front of Ivan, directly below the site of the apparition. As Ivan fixed his eyes on the invisible presence of the Mother of God, Linda prayed simply to the "Gospa"[9] to heal her little girl or take her home to heaven. As soon as the apparition had ended, Ivan went over and knelt down next to Audrey. He proceeded to speak to her in Croatian for about five minutes. No one with Audrey could understand what he was saying. Three days later, on August 4, Linda, Joyce, and Audrey returned to the choir loft for a second apparition. Audrey was once again placed on the floor, though this time she appeared calm and quiet, even refreshed

---

[8] There has been no official decision from the Catholic Church on the nature of the events in Medjugorje. The story we relate here is one of private testimony only. The author and publisher submit entirely to the Church's direction and teaching concerning Medjugorje.

[9] Name for the Blessed Virgin Mary used by the people of Medjugorje

despite the stifling heat in the choir loft. The apparition lasted a full twenty minutes or more. Afterwards, Ivan once again spoke with Audrey, but no one could hear or understand what was said.

Nothing dramatic had happened during either of the apparitions; however, a few hours following the second apparition, Audrey's condition changed radically. It seemed at first that the hoped for miracle was happening. Her head and hands began to move and her pupils equalized and reacted to the light. Her eyes followed her nurse, Joyce. Then, suddenly, Audrey went into cardiac arrest. The miracle turned into a nightmare. On the spot, Audrey was resuscitated. Then followed a roller coaster ride of finding adequate medical care in an impoverished and backward country. During the long drive to and from different medical facilities, Audrey's heart stopped and she had to be resuscitated five times. Then, when she was finally stabilized, no airliner would accept the responsibility of carrying her home for fear that she would expire en route. Due to the intervention of Massachusetts Congressman Joseph Early, the Air Force special-detail plane "Med-Star" stationed in Frankfurt, Germany, was able to pick up the little troupe in Yugoslavia and get them back to the States.

In August 1988, just a few weeks after the return from Medjugorje, Audrey began showing mysterious physical manifestations. An examining physician was startled by the appearance of red marks on Audrey's palms. These marks would appear and disappear sporadically, sometimes on one hand, sometimes on the other, sometimes on both. Over time, the red marks became more pronounced, taking the form of holes that would mysteriously appear and then just as mysteriously close. Later that fall, red stripe marks began to appear covering Audrey's face, upper body, and arms. She looked like she had been flogged. Sometime in January 1989, Audrey's right foot began to exhibit something similar to the marks on her hands. No clinical explanation could be found for these markings.

Audrey also began to exhibit the "phenomena of weight." This term refers to a condition noted with visionaries and mystics who have entered into an altered state of consciousness. Weighing less than thirty pounds, Audrey would suddenly arch her back and become immovable. At the same time, her pulse would rise from a normal 80-90 beats per minute to 185-200 beats per minute. Audrey could remain in this condition for as long as eight hours – a medical impossibility.

Things really came to a head in Lent of 1989. Audrey was apparently living the passion in intense pain and suffering. She had to be hospitalized – but nothing was found to be the cause of her crying and agony. Finally, at 3:00 P.M. on Good Friday, she fell into a deep sleep.

A Treasury of Mystical Happenings

In the weeks following Easter 1989, other kinds of manifestations began to bear witness to the importance of this little suffering soul. From that time until the present, the Santo home has been a gold mine of mystical events.

Bishop Timothy J. Harrington, D.D., Ordinary of the Diocese of Worcester from 1983-1994, granted permission for a tabernacle to be placed in Audrey's room. Even before the dramatic events of Lent 1989, statues in Audrey's room were noted to have turned on their own to face the tabernacle, and rosaries and chaplets had turned gold. Holy water sprinkled on Audrey would glitter and sparkle. After

Easter of that year, these events began to proliferate. An image of Our Lady of Guadalupe poured out oil that filled the room with the smell of roses. Other icons and pictures in the house began to exude oil. A picture of St. Rita of Cascia, a gift from the people of Lebanon, wept blood. The statue of the Rosa Mystica shed real tears.

Word got out about the astounding events surrounding little Audrey. People began coming to the Santo home to see for themselves what was happening and to ask little Audrey to pray for them. A friend of the Santo family who had received a special blessing through the intercession of little Audrey converted their garage into a chapel where Mass could be said for the family and visiting pilgrims. In 1990, oil began dripping from items in the chapel, including the Sacramentary (the book containing the prayers of the Mass).

Four hosts have bled in the Santo home and chapel. The first occurred on January 15, 1992. This host had been consecrated by the late Bishop Bernard Flanagan (at that time retired) and reposed within the tabernacle in Audrey's room. Similarly, in 1995, two other hosts, consecrated this time by Father George Joyce during Mass at the Santo home, were discovered to have bled as they lay within the tabernacle. The only host to actually bleed on the altar during a Mass was the one I was privileged to witness on June 5, 1996.[10]

What is happening in little Audrey's home is at the present time in the hands of the local ordinary, Bishop Daniel P. Reilly. Under his direction, diocesan officials are

---

[10] This event was captured on video: *Audrey's Life: Voice of a Silent Soul*, available at: The Mercy Foundation, P.O. Box 383, Mundelein, IL, 60060. Phone : (847) 247-8170 / Fax : (847) 367-7831.

continuing to submit the phenomena in the Santo house to professional and scientific analysis. Dr. Robert Ciottone, J.C.D., Dr. John Maddonna, Head of the Commission, and Father F. Stephen Pedone, Vicar of the Worcester Diocese, were appointed by Bishop Reilly to be the investigative team. The resulting report ruled out "chicanery" and stressed that Audrey was loved and well cared for by her parents, Steve and Linda Santo. With some questions still left unanswered, the diocese ordered further inquiry. Teams have spent time at the Santo home, including some nights, and have interviewed those closest to the little girl who provide her with round-the-clock care. They also plan to set up infrared-photography equipment in little Audrey's room. In short, no stone is being left unturned.

Yet, mystery continues to surround little Audrey. The oils have proven to be of an organic nature and include an unknown compound. Tests conducted on the blood of the hosts has verified that it is human and does not match that of any member of the family. No evidence of hoax has been found. When Lynn Scherr of *20/20* asked the investigators point blank what conclusion they had reached concerning the happenings in the Santo residence, their answer was, "Inexplicable."

Team psychologist John Maddonna said, "We found nothing we could consider to be trickery. Our role is to study the observable, not miracles."[11]

The diocese has made no final judgment; rather, it has pointed to the love and care little Audrey receives as the most important lesson to be derived from her story. Bishop

---

[11] Boston Herald, Friday 1/22/1999, pg. 16.

Reilly has stated, "Only the diocese, if necessary the Vatican, can officially speak on the Church's position regarding little Audrey Santo. The most striking presence of God in the Santo home is the dedication of the family to Audrey . . . and the most constant miracle . . . is that at Mass, water and wine become the Body and Blood of Christ."[12]

Within Audrey's family, another kind of miracle occurred. In 1995, Steve and Linda began to make their way towards reconciliation. On June 24, 1996, they renewed their wedding vows.

Little Audrey's ministry has touched the lives of thousands of people. Over the years, the anniversary of her fall into the family pool has become a day of pilgrimage and prayer. The August 11, 1997, edition of the Worcester *Telegram & Gazette* described the event at Christ the King Church, the Santos' parish:

> *Thousands of people crammed the sanctuary, basement and grounds of Christ the King Church yesterday for a Mass for and a glimpse of Audrey Santo, a thirteen-year old Flagg Street girl who has been in a coma since she was three years old.*
>
> *"It's a little overwhelming," said Jennifer K. Baker, Santo's older sister. "Two-thousand people were here last year, and now it's close to five thousand." They came to the city in cars, buses and planes, some to pray for Audrey's recovery, some to seek blessings for themselves or loved ones, and some out of curiosity . . . Saturday marked the tenth anniversary of the day Audrey was pulled unconscious from the family swimming pool .*

---

[12] See Appendix III for the diocese's official statement concerning Audrey Santo.

. . "And here we are celebrating life ten years later,"
Baker said.

More than thirty chartered buses, unloading passengers
outside the church, and the hoards of vehicles delayed
traffic along Pleasant Street for blocks during the early
part of the afternoon. Six hundred people sat through the
service in the church sanctuary, while another three
hundred watched it on a large-screen television
downstairs. Speakers and monitors also were set up in
the grass outside the church where most of the crowd
remained.

After the Mass, visitors lined up to view Audrey, who
could be seen through the window of a small room just
inside the entry to the sanctuary.

Baker said the annual Mass began as a small family
observance, but recent publicity has brought people from
around the world to see her sister. "She is bringing
people closer to God, not only Catholics, but from faiths
all over," she said.

In 1998, the numbers at the commemorative Mass
reached eight to ten thousand. To accommodate such a great
crowd, Mass was held at Holy Cross Stadium.

Little Audrey has garnered the praise and admiration of
many respected Church figures. Healer Father Charles
Babbit has referred to her as "a living saint." Father
Sylvester Catallo, O.F.M. Cap., the American translator for
the Marian Movement of Priests founder Don Stefano Gobbi,
considers little Audrey a "pure" victim soul since she has
probably never committed a mortal sin, having suffered her
accident at the tender age of four. Father Immanuel Charles

McCarthy (no relation), the Melkite priest whose daughter's miraculous cure was the final step in the canonization of St. Edith Stein, sees in little Audrey a redemptive sacrifice for sins of nuclear destruction. He points to interesting parallels between significant dates and events in little Audrey's life and the dropping of the bomb on Hiroshima and Nagasaki. The highly regarded French theologian Rene Laurentin made a special visit to little Audrey in July 1993 and wrote about her with great enthusiasm. He said of her home, "This is holy ground."

The most widely held opinion about little Audrey is that she is living as a "silent soul." We know that there is only one mediator between God and man, Jesus Christ; however, we also believe that God has allowed the faithful to participate in the salvific work of His Son in different ways and degrees. St. Paul says, "I make up for in my body what is lacking in the suffering of Christ." That is not to say that the passion, death, and resurrection of the Lord are in any way deficient! St. Paul simply wants us to understand that we are united to Christ through baptism in such a way that our sufferings and those of the Lord are one. A silent soul lives this mystery in a particular way by knowingly and willingly offering himself or herself to God in reparation for sin and the salvation of souls. Those who have experienced the miraculous events surrounding little Audrey believe that she has accepted this vocation and made an offering of herself to God. The efficacy of little Audrey's intercession is acclaimed by many, while heaven itself seems determined to ratify her apostolate with innumerable signs and wonders.

Meeting Audrey

In 1990, thanks to the insistence of my brother Vincent and his wife Ginny, I walked into the incredible story of little Audrey Santo.

My first visit is forever etched on my mind. Vincent, Ginny and I drove first to Worcester and had lunch at a local restaurant. We then worked our way over to South Flagg Street and parked the car near the Santo house.[13]

Since my brother and his wife were good friends of the Santos, they were allowed to accompany me directly into little Audrey's room. We prayed and visited with her.[14] Then Vincent, Ginny and I went into the chapel where a number of people were already gathered for Mass. The first thing that caught my eye was a large cloth picture of Our Lady of Guadalupe in a wooden frame, about six feet by three feet. I went up to look at it and noticed two streams of oil coming down from the left eye of the image. This was my first experience with an oil-bleeding image. I didn't know what to think. I was skeptical. I thought at first that it had to be some kind of illusion or mirage. Then I went into the sacristy to vest for Mass and met Father George Joyce for the first time. He was at that time spiritual director of the Santo family. He would be the main celebrant at my first Mass in the Santo chapel, just as he would be six years later on the occasion of the bleeding host.

---

[13] This is no longer possible. Today, if you wish to visit the chapel, you must park on the main street and walk over to 64 South Flagg Street.

[14] As of February 1999, lay people are no longer permitted this privilege. Only priests are allowed a personal visit with Audrey.

No extraordinary phenomena occurred during the Mass other than the continuing presence of oil on the sacred objects and vessels. As I looked around me, I noticed that there were two twelve by twelve pieces of glass on either side of the altar. Both of these were sticky with oil, but the oil didn't seem to be dripping off the glass. The front cover of the Sacramentary (the book containing the prayers of the Mass) was saturated with oil, and various other items on the altar were dripping with oil. The paten also was covered with a thick oily film. Even the chalice was sticky with oil inside and outside. This was particularly noticeable when we poured the wine into the chalice since the oil could be seen floating on top of the wine. When we drank from the cup at communion time, I could taste the oil mixed with the wine.

After Mass, we visited with Linda Santo, Audrey, and the rest of the family and volunteers. Little Audrey could not talk or move a muscle. She could only flash and move her eyes and make a little movement in her left hand. We stayed until Ginny's oxygen started running low and we had to return to South Boston.

Though I was skeptical about the strange things I had seen, this first visit to little Audrey's home had made an impression on me. I was especially touched by the peace I felt there.

After I was transferred back to Arlington Heights to serve as coordinator of the Viatorian Retirement Center, I came back to South Boston every summer to visit my family. On these occasions, I stayed at Sts. Peter and Paul rectory where I always had a room available. On Wednesdays, Vincent, Ginny and I would go to Worcester to see little Audrey and participate in the 1:00 P.M. Mass. This was my routine up to and including June 5, 1996. Consequently, I had been a very frequent visitor at the Santo residence long before that eventful day in June.

Why did I keep going back?

The simplicity of this treasure-trove of miracles spoke to me more than anything else. Little Audrey's home is an ordinary, middle-class, ranch type house on a small street in a typical New England town. The one-car-garage-turned-chapel is nothing spectacular. Its ornaments are hung in a sporadic, one could even say, haphazard way. It lacks the grandeur of the basilicas where famous mystical events have taken place – places like Fatima or Lourdes, or even Medjugorje. Yet, notwithstanding the disheveled decor, when you walk into the chapel, you feel that you have entered another realm. Sometimes the scent of roses hangs in the air. The bleeding of oil from various pictures, crucifixes and statues speaks "mystery." Every place where Jesus is present in the tabernacle is a holy place, but in the Santo chapel, the concrete reminders that God is present cut through our "business as usual" approach to stepping into a church. Even for me, a priest, visiting the chapel and saying Mass there is a re-awakening of my faith and a deepening of my relationship with my Heavenly Father.

So, I kept going back to see little Audrey. How could I stay away? Heaven had touched me through this little girl and the astounding events that were happening in her home. We all long to see the face of God. As Scripture says, "My soul thirsts for God, for the living God. When shall I come and behold the face of God?" (Ps 42:2). Though I may have visited little Audrey the first time to satisfy Vincent and Ginny and my own curiosity, later I went to quench my own spiritual thirst. I was a pilgrim, like every other pilgrim who visited the house on South Flagg Street. I was nobody special. After all, the story was little Audrey's, not mine.

Out of the Rocking Chair

I suppose you would expect that after experiencing something as extraordinary as a bleeding host a person would show an immediate and radical difference in lifestyle. Sadly, I have to say that in my case it wasn't long before the memory of this event was overshadowed by ordinary routine and a lack of enthusiasm from others.

One tiny light still glimmered on the horizon. I eagerly awaited the Mercy Foundation's videotape on the life of Audrey, knowing that it would include footage of the bleeding host. The videotape would be available in November 1996. I looked forward to seeing it and sharing it with everyone at the retirement center. The expectation of seeing the bleeding host event recorded on film kept the experience fresh in my memory even though everyday life seemed to have returned to normal.

The tape was no disappointment. It captured the actual moment when the host began to bleed and the sounds and looks of astonishment from all of us in the chapel, in particular, we priests on the altar. Watching all this on video stirred up many mixed emotions in me. On the one hand, it was incredible to see myself witnessing the bleeding host and to hear my words to John Clote after the Mass. I felt once again the joy of this magnificent expression of God's love for me. At the same time, there was something surreal about it all. The tape made me an observer to my own experience. I could see myself, but I couldn't believe that it was really me standing next to Father George as he held that bleeding host high in the air. If it hadn't actually been recorded on film, I don't think I could have believed that God had really chosen me to witness such an extraordinary event. In any case, I had again that funny feeling that something was supposed to come of all this, though I couldn't say what or how.

Foolishly, I assumed that the video of the bleeding host would make my brother priests jump up and down with joy. In my mind, a bleeding host was an event that had consequences for all of us priests. In addition, this had happened to one of their own Viatorians right here in the United States – not some far away place overseas. Little Audrey Santo was still living there in Worcester, still surrounded by countless signs and miracles. This was a "now" event, given by heaven for us today. I felt so excited as I gathered everyone around the VCR. My words didn't have to stand alone anymore; I had proof on the video. I was full of anticipation about how my confreres would react. I had waited patiently for this moment.

My brother priests watched the video with interest, but if I had been hoping for some kind of profound response, I was disappointed.

I was very depressed. I had waited so long to share my experience with my brothers, partly in the hope that with their help I would understand what direction, if any, I should take. But that didn't happen. None of them suggested any kind of expansion in my life, any kind of fruit that might or should come from having received such a grace. I knew that something extraordinary had happened to me, and that something was supposed to follow such an experience, but obviously I was not able to cope with the awesome nature of the event. I didn't know who to talk to, nor did I seek advice from anyone. I was completely alone.

I shouldn't be so hard on my brothers. In the end I wasn't any different from the rest of the priests in the house. I had no clue what to do with it all, so I just let it go. After a spurt of enthusiasm over the videotape, I just sat in my easy chair and began rocking my way to eternity. Okay, that's not entirely truthful. I can say that I stayed busy, but I was just in a holding pattern, repeating the same circle of activities that I had built up over a lifetime: Marriage Encounter and Retrouvaille weekends, Knights of Columbus activities, fiddling and bowling and golfing. Nothing new. And that's how I thought it was going to stay.

I guess God knew I couldn't walk this path alone. He had already foreseen and planned the next step on this incredible journey. Right around the corner a friend was waiting to help me bring this magnificent experience to fruition.

In the spring of 1997, I received a call from a stranger, a certain Gina Friend, who was calling not only for herself but for her friends Harriet Lechleider and Joe Fitzpatrick, a professor at Northwestern University. Gina did the talking. She wanted to know if I were the same Father McCarthy in the Mercy Foundation videotape about little Audrey Santo. I said yes. She could hardly speak for excitement. She told me that she and her friends would like to have lunch with me and talk about what they had seen on the videotape, something they felt was unique, marvelous, and extraordinary.

The four of us eventually came together at the Palm Court Restaurant in Arlington Heights. It was a beautiful day. The sun was shining and I was feeling great wondering what these people were stewing up for me. More than I could have imagined! It would be no lie to say that without Gina and Harriet I would not be writing these pages now. I would still be sitting in my rocking chair in Arlington Heights. These two ladies lifted me up and inspired me to go into another ministry at the ripe old age of seventy-seven. How did they do it? Their excitement was contagious. They could hardly control themselves in my presence. Just being *near* a priest who had actually seen the Son of God in a bleeding host was, for them, a grace and a wonder. I was moved to tears by their faith. I couldn't believe that someone really recognized and shared with me the magnitude of what I had witnessed. Everything that I had kept locked up in my heart could suddenly pour out freely.

I'll give the floor to Gina now to tell in her own words what this meeting meant:

*In June of 1997, a girlfriend sent me a videotape of Little Audrey Santo . . . As I watched the video with awesome wonder . . . it reinforced in my mind how **truly present Jesus is in the Eucharist**. Why [hadn't] we heard about Father Tom talking and spreading the word around here? I had this **urgent feeling** to call him. I called my friend Harriet Lechleider and asked her how I could locate this priest. I noticed on the film that he lived in Arlington Heights, Illinois − two to three miles from where I live! She asked me if I got the initials behind his name. I said, "No." She said look again, and I saw St.*

Viator's in Arlington Heights — her kids went to that school! This was no coincidence — this was God's plan — something was about to happen. The Holy Spirit was moving fast.

Four phone calls later, I was speaking personally with Father Tom McCarthy . . . How excited we were to be able to meet Father Tom, a special priest, chosen from many, to see this special miracle of the Eucharist. As we pulled up to St. Viator's, we were expecting to meet another Moses. What we saw was a very thin, frail looking, six-foot two-inch man wearing a light tan short trench coat that didn't exactly fit, blue trousers, and a colored cap! So much for Moses! But we were anxious to meet him. We knew he was special to be chosen to witness Jesus, truly present in a bleeding host . . . very special indeed.

As I looked at him, I had to know what was behind that sad looking face. We bombarded this quiet, frail, humble priest with questions and he finally began to open up. He hesitated at first to tell his story — that he was seventy-seven years old, that he was the eldest of eleven children . . . that his alcoholic father had deserted the family . . . [about] his hopes of becoming a priest . . .

A few days later, I called Father Tom and asked if he would concelebrate a Mass and walk in procession with the Blessed Sacrament and the Rosa Mystica statue around the grounds at St. Joseph's in Lake Zurich. All the special children at St. Joseph's knelt as they watched in awe as the procession passed by. This statue of the Rosa Mystica then wept tears for days at St. John of the Cross Church in Chicago!

*Little did Father Tom realize what the next three years would enfold – God's plan was at work. We booked Father Tom everywhere – churches, conferences, private homes, and he is booked through the end of the year 2000. At the age of eighty, he is in high gear – spreading the **Good News of Jesus, truly present in the Eucharist.***

Gina is one of the prime movers of the prayer group at the Divine Word's Holy Spirit Chapel on Waukegan & Techny Roads in Northbrook, Illinois. The members of the prayer group had been deeply moved by the Mercy Foundation video and wanted to know more about what happened that day at the Santo home. On behalf of Father Leo Hotze, S.V.D., Gina invited me to come give a talk before the Mass on one of their Wednesday night gatherings. I had my reservations about telling my story to a group of people, but Gina kept saying over and over, "Father Tom, you just have to go out and spread the message of the true presence of Jesus in the Holy Eucharist." How could I refuse?

There was a big crowd that night; the whole church was filled. Mostly these were people who had been or were going to go to Medjugorje. They were a spirit-filled group and it was wonderful to be among them. I spoke about little Audrey Santo and the bleeding host that I had witnessed. I also described the other mysterious events at the Santo home, the other hosts that bled while in the tabernacle, and the bleeding of oil from religious images and altar furnishings.

I can't say it was easy that first night. I knew that I was not a polished speaker. True to form, I was once again beginning something without any preparation. Sure, I had spent years in the classroom, but that's hardly the same thing as giving a personal witness before an audience of adults. You remember how afraid I was to give that Midnight Mass homily in Reno? Well, I hadn't changed much over the years. And what about my retreat work, you may ask? Wasn't I used to giving talks? Yes and no. The intimacy of a Marriage Encounter weekend was one thing, but to actually hit the lecture circuit . . . hold on!

I suppose I had it in the back of my mind that this was going to be a one-shot deal. I certainly never planned on turning a single night of witness into a lifestyle, but that is what happened. Through Gina and Harriet, I entered upon a new vocation giving talks to prayer groups and conferences about what I had witnessed of the Real Presence in the Eucharist. At an age when I should have been packing it up with the other priests at the retirement center, I was starting from scratch in a new apostolate. I was about to learn the full meaning of the phrase "a priest forever." Like the great baseball manager said, "It's not over 'til it's over."

I'm not saying that I leaped lightly into this new life. I knew that I was no public speaker, but fortunately the Holy Spirit eased me into my new vocation by having me give short talks to small prayer groups in the Arlington Heights area. Gradually, I learned to cope with stage fright and even warm up to an audience.

The Holy Spirit also provided friends for me who would make up for my failings. I entered a new kind of family, one that would grow by leaps and bounds in the weeks, months, and years to come. If Gina liked to think of me as her "Moses," I have to say that in her the Holy Spirit gave me my "Aaron." She made the contacts and opened doors to speaking engagements. She kept me on schedule and made sure I got from place to place. On a comic note, Gina and

Harriet also made me "road worthy." They had their work cut out for them. I was a seventy-seven year old religious priest with the entrenched habits of a bachelor accustomed to a life of poverty.

I may be the front man, but the real heroes are Gina and Harriet. Over the years I have grown to know and admire these two women. Gina's name actually comes from Regina Marie, the name her mother chose for her because she was born on the Feast of the Holy Rosary, October 7. Gina is a cancer survivor. Fourteen years ago she was preparing to meet God face-to-face when she experienced a physical and spiritual healing. As she says, "I am grateful to our Dear Lord – He picked me up and made me whole. I have become Catholic again and Jesus has been the center of my life since. He has graced me with many wonders." Gina's enthusiasm for her faith is unbounded. She loves to be at the center of things. A born organizer, she has all kinds of things going on at her table at the entrance to the church. Her country-style outfits and dish-color blonde hair fit her outgoing personality. She is also a very giving person who cares for a sister in a nursing home.

Harriet and Gina are best friends. They are quite a pair. They are always kidding and uplifting each other. Harriet is always in a jovial mood. Nothing seems to bother her. She is a petite lady and an up-to-date, fashionable dresser with a striking head of red hair. Harriet and her husband are true apostles of the Real Presence; there isn't anything they won't do to spread devotion to the Lord in the Eucharist. This reaches heroic proportions sometimes since Harriet suffers continually from bone problems – she is always falling or breaking something. She has also endured several bypass surgeries.*

Between Gina and Harriet, I was kept busy on a series of speaking engagements in the local area, everything from parish Masses, to prayer group talks, to private home meetings, to radio appearances. Gina had one goal: Get the word out!

The fruit of these visits was very gratifying, but Gina felt that I had to take my story to an even bigger audience. She got in touch with Larry and Mary Sue Eck, editors of *The Medjugorje Magazine*. They, in turn, asked me to say Mass at the Catholic Shoppe in Westmont, Illinois. Following this event, Mary Sue invited me to speak at the mini-Marian Conference that was to be held at the Odeum sports arena in Villa Park, Illinois, on November 14-15, 1997.

This was a huge event, way outside of the kind of simple parish groups that I had done so far. I was scared. The people coming to the mini-Marian Conference were expecting professional speakers. I was a nobody. I thought that once I got started most people would get up and leave and I would be embarrassed. This was the big time, and I didn't know if I was ready for it. I looked forward to the event with some trepidation, let me tell you.

Finally, the moment arrived. I was the last person scheduled to speak on the Friday night of the conference. Just before my time came, I was doing my thing hearing confessions at the back of the auditorium. Then I heard my

---

* As I was writing these words, the Lord called Harriet Lechleider home. We celebrate her birth into heaven, though we dearly miss her on earth.

name called and I came rushing down to give my talk. I had my stole on over my black suit. I said a quick prayer to the Holy Spirit to speak through me. Mary Sue Eck gave me a nice introduction. Then she and Larry each gave me a hug. That gave me confidence. I sure needed it. When I turned to face the audience, the lights were so strong that I could not see the people's faces. I couldn't tell how they were reacting to what I was telling them. I just went ahead in faith.

I read my prepared talk, but I did some ad-libbing a few times. When I told the people about going to Worcester from the direction of South Boston, I pointed out that you have to go west – if you go east you will land in the ocean – and if that happens, you will need a rowboat. I wasn't really trying to be funny, but the people loved it and started laughing. That bolstered me up a bit. In the end, I had the people not only laughing, but crying. When I finished, they gave me a nice round of applause. I guess they liked it. According to Mary Sue Eck, I was a success, and she must really have thought so because she published my talk in the 1998 Spring issue of *The Medjugorje Magazine.*

For New Year's Eve 1997, Gina Friend invited me to attend the celebration at Mount Saint Joseph Home in Lake Zurich, Illinois. We had adoration of the Blessed Sacrament, followed by Scripture reading. Then I gave a talk on my experience of events at the Santo home.

In January 1998, I was asked to participate in the Real Presence Conference in Vandalia, Illinois. The conference was sponsored by Mother of Dolors Church and held in the Vandalia High School Auditorium. I was invited to attend by Father Stephen Sotiroff, pastor of Mother Dolors, and his pastoral assistants Debbie Pryor and Vanessa Keck. This time I didn't have to do any public speaking. I was given a special room where I could set up a display on little Audrey and the bleeding hosts and be ready to speak about my experiences to people who came by during the course of the weekend. Gina and Harriet provided me with transportation to Vandalia and stayed with me throughout the conference. Gina had already seen to the enlargement and framing of the photos we would use. The two main pictures we were showing off were of the bleeding host that I had witnessed on June 5, 1996, during Mass, and the four bleeding hosts which are reposed in the tabernacle in little Audrey's room. I believe that those who came to view this exhibit went away with a stronger feeling for the sacredness of Jesus in the Eucharist.

During the weekend of October 2-4, 1998, I returned once again to Vandalia at the invitation of Debbie Pryor and Vanessa Keck to attend the Marian Pro-life conference. This time about six hundred people were in attendance.

The prayer group at St. Edwards Church, Rockford, Illinois, also invited me to share my experiences. Gina, Harriet, and Harriet's husband Dick drove me to Rockford on November 8, 1998. By this time, I had been able to accompany Gina and Harriet to little Audrey's home. During the talk I invited them to give their version of what they had seen there. The audience was very touched by the witness of all three of us together.

In the midst of all this, I received a special grace during a visit to retired Bishop Alfred L. Abramowicz who was in residence at the rectory of St. Blase Church. Elaine Doerrfeld, a close friend of Gina's, called to ask if we could visit the bishop, who was very ill at the time, and talk to him about little Audrey. A few days later, I was sitting by his side telling him about the bleeding host and showing him a photo of the four hosts that have bled at little Audrey's home and that are kept in the tabernacle in her room. The bishop sat up in bed, held the picture very close to his face, and said in a deeply haunting, reverent whisper, "Frightening, frightening!" I then blessed him with the oil from little Audrey's home and prayed with him for awhile.

Suddenly, he bellowed out a command to "get the stole, get the stole!" and instructed Father Norbert Waszak, pastor of St. Blase, where to find it in his room. The rest of us had no idea what was going on. Father Norb returned with a plastic green bag, from which he pulled out an old stole. The bishop motioned for me to put it around my shoulders, and as I did so he told me, "This is the confessional stole of St. John Vianney." It was a great privilege and blessing for me as a priest to wear the stole of the famous Curé of Ars. Bishop Abramowicz had received the stole from an army chaplain who served in France during the last world war. The American soldiers in his outfit had given money to help a pastor of a church in need where they were stationed. The pastor offered the stole to the chaplain in thanksgiving for their help; subsequently, the chaplain gave the stole to the bishop. I believe the stole went to Mundelein Seminary in Illinois after the bishop passed away.

In the Fall of 1999, I received a call from Joan and Tom McHugh to be part of a day of recollection at Marytown Retreat Center, Libertyville, Illinois, on December 8. The McHughs are the editors of *The Witness*, the magazine of their apostolate to foster devotion to the Real Presence of Christ in the Holy Eucharist. Since, you could say, we are in the same business, I had no problem accepting the invitation! I said Mass for the day of recollection and talked about my experience of the bleeding host. Everyone was listening attentively. Joan was so pleased with my presentation that she invited me to be on the same program with her for a retreat in Indiana.

On December 12, 1999, the Feast of Our Lady of Guadalupe, I was one of the speakers for a day of prayer and healing in preparation for the new millennium sponsored by the Two Hearts Healing Ministry in Darien, Illinois. A fair sized crowd had gathered for the day – all former pilgrims to Medjugorje.

I also gave talks on my experiences with little Audrey and the bleeding host to the St. James Men's Club at St. James Parish in Arlington Heights which meets every second Wednesday of the month, and to the group of men who meet once a month on Saturday morning. About fifty men were present for each presentation.

In March 2000, Ed Condon, Secretary of the Chicago Association of Holy Name Societies, invited me to give a talk at Transfiguration Church in Chicago, Illinois. The church was nearly filled and the talk went over well.

In April 2000, I was invited again by Joan Carter McHugh to join in giving a "Life in the Eucharist" retreat at the Lindenwood Retreat Center in Donaldson, Indiana. I said the Masses for these two days and gave three presentations, including one of witness to the Real Presence in the bleeding host.

Over time, I have improved the quality of my presentation. I might have been slow getting out of the gate, but I have gradually picked up momentum. Gina and I worked in some photos that she had blown up to an eight by eleven size. Using an electric spot pointer (high tech!), I am able to get down from the podium and point to the picture while describing the photo extemporaneously. I know I have grown as a speaker because I have the confidence to do this. I am no longer glued to the written word.

As part of my talk, I also share a little about my life. In the telling of the tale, I have come to appreciate that my whole life, not just June 5, 1996, bears witness to God's love for me and can serve to strengthen the faith of others. It's amazing how people react to my story. Here is a letter from Mayor Michael O'Malley of the Village of Hoffman Estates, Illinois, which he sent me a few months before his untimely death in September 2000:

> 6-11-00
>
> Dear Father McCarthy
>
> I had the great pleasure of being at the Mass you said at St. Hubert's on June 4, 2000. I must tell you, I don't know of any Mass that I've ever been at that did more to lift my spirits than that one. When you spoke of your mother it opened a flood of memories of my own mom. I was in dire need of that. Thank you so much. Sometimes we lose touch with the past. God bless you for taking me back.
>
> Mike O'Malley

I was once again invited to attend the annual conference of Our Sorrowful Mother's Ministry in Vandalia the weekend of October 27-29, 2000. The weekend was emceed by Zip Rzeppa of Catholic radio station WRYT out of St. Louis, Missouri. I couldn't believe I was on a program that included such famous names as Father John Corapi, S.O.L.T., Father Bill Casey, C.P.M., Father Jordan Aumann, O.P., Father Philip Scott, Father Ken Hummel, and Father Peter West, not to mention singer/songwriter Annie Karto from Florida who, along with Tina Marie and John Robert Hanna, provided the music ministry for the three days.

I know there are a lot of questions surrounding the happenings at the Santo home. I know there's a lot of discussion about what "victim soul" means. But finding the answers to these questions is not my department. I'm no theologian. As a religious priest, I am bound to preserve the teaching of the Catholic Church and stay obedient to my superior and my bishop. I try to do that. When I speak about the bleeding host, all I'm doing is telling what I saw. It's a personal story. I don't want it to be taken for anything more than that and I don't try to present it as anything other than that. I'm not trying to sell anything to anyone or convince anyone of anything. I just tell it like it happened.

A Priest Forever

Come and See!

We are so blessed to have little Audrey Santo in this country. We hear so much about what happened at Lourdes and Fatima, and what is happening now in Medjugorje, but right here in the USA we have a prodigy, maybe one of the greatest in the history of our faith. She is a special gift of God to our country. No matter where I roam or to whom I speak, the little ranch-style house in Worcester, Massachusetts, remains at the center of my story. I am happy to say that part of my apostolate has been to bring people directly to the source. And every time I take people to little Audrey's home, I see miracles. I see the lives of visitors change from this personal contact with little Audrey and the wonders happening in her home chapel.

Of all my trips to Worcester, that which is dearest to my heart is the one I shared with Gina and Harriet in December 1997. These two women had dedicated themselves to spreading devotion to the Real Presence, particularly through the story of little Audrey and the bleeding host. How could I resist their request to see for themselves what they had heard me so often describe? We only had time for a fast and furious trip, and nothing extraordinary happened, but it seemed that on this occasion we were all gifted with a special experience of the peace of heaven.

Our trip certainly didn't start out easy. We left the hotel near Logan Airport in Boston and Harriet rented a car. The cold weather caused the windshield to fog up and, while Harriet tried to keep her eyes on the road, I made a fruitless search for the defogging button. We were forced to open the windows and poor Gina in the backseat was soon frozen. Rather bedraggled, we arrived at Christ the King Church where the Mass and celebration were going to be held. Since we arrived about noon, somewhat early for Mass, I suggested we go down to Audrey's home. Steve Santo let us in and we visited with Audrey.

I'll let Gina describe what she felt that day:

We had seen the film on Audrey and were in awe of the mysterious events happening in that little house in Worcester, Massachusetts. Curiosity and excitement filled our hearts as we approached the Santo home. Mr. Santo kindly welcomed us inside, and we were led to Audrey's room. A rare occasion, just the three of us alone with Audrey except for a nurse at her side. Usually the house is crowded with people, but this day everyone was gathering at Christ the King Church to celebrate the Mass for Audrey for her birthday. They were planning to take Audrey to the Church later.

It was unbelievable that we were here in this room. Her room was filled wall to wall with holy pictures, statues, crucifixes, and gifts from people from all over the world. All had at one time wept tears, oil, and even blood. My eyes caught the sight of a tabernacle to the left of her bed that contains the four hosts that bled. We were overcome with a profound presence of a big God and were immersed in a deep state of a mysterious silence – a silence of awe and disbelief of not being there. Jesus was sacramentally present in that house, in that room, with Audrey, with us. A feeling of holiness surrounded the three of us.

Father Tom bent over this child and blessed her – her eyes danced lovingly at him. Harriet and I held her hand and she again talked with her eyes. I wondered what she might be thinking – perhaps just a simple hello. As a mother, I felt my heart cry with helplessness as I gazed at this little child lying there. Then my eyes were drawn toward the tabernacle and I knew He was in our midst, His peace consoled us. Little Audrey is in God's hands twenty-four hours a day. He will take care of her. The three of us then moved quietly to the little chapel, in that little garage at the end of that little house.

Suddenly things started moving fast. Linda came in to say the paramedics were coming to take Audrey up to the church for the celebration. We made ourselves scarce.

I took Gina and Harriet into the chapel. The atmosphere that day was even more charged than normally. The quiet and stillness didn't diminish the feeling of expectation that always hangs in the air there. We all felt this together. Here we were, the three of us, surrounded by mystery. Pictures and statues dripping oil – the chalice on the altar filling continually with oil – the Mass book with its cover just saturated with oil. Extraordinary! We had the sensation of being plunged into a Holy Place. We were experiencing heaven on earth. I have heard that many people who go to Medjugorje experience a peacefulness that is indescribable.

That's how the three of us were feeling. Just experiencing a little bit of heaven in little Audrey's chapel in Worcester, Massachusetts.

Gina also shared these sentiments:

As we entered the chapel . . . we saw wall-to-wall pictures, plaques, and crucifixes – markings of dripping oil on the pictures, cups catching oil dripping from crucifixes – everything sticky with dripping oil. My God! What was going on here? Not just one, not just two, but almost everything looked shiny with oil – I had to wonder if even we were dripping with oil!

Father Tom pointed to a crucifix on the left side of the altar. The crucifix was dripping oil in front of our eyes into a paper cup that was already half full. Then Father Tom lifted up a gold chalice on the altar in this chapel and touched it – oil formed on his fingers – the chalice was wet with oil! Here before us was a sea of wonders, all in one place – a humble little home on a dead-end street somewhere outside of Boston.

We then went up to Christ the King Church. After the Mass, we all went downstairs for little Audrey's fourteenth birthday party. Only certain people were invited to this gathering – just family and a few volunteers who looked after the needs of little Audrey's home and the Apostolate of a Silent Soul. Afterward, we returned to Arlington Heights.

In January 1998, Debbie Pryor and Vanessa Keck, the pastoral assistants for Mother Dolors Catholic Church in Vandalia, Illinois, asked me if they could go with me sometime to visit little Audrey. I had spoken several times in Vandalia at their invitation. They had been impressed by what they heard and wanted to see for themselves. I was to be home in South Boston anyway for a family get-together in April, so we agreed to meet and travel together to the Santo home. On April 22, 1998, Vanessa and Debbie flew to Providence, Rhode Island, rented a car, and then checked into a motel near Worcester, Massachusetts. They picked me up at Sts. Peter and Paul rectory where I was staying in South Boston, and we drove to Worcester.

Every time I visit the Santo home something special happens. This day was no exception. We followed the usual procedure when we arrived: we left the car at Christ the King Church parking lot and took the shuttle the rest of the way to the Santo residence. We discovered about sixty people there already. One of the volunteers gave the visitors a brief account of little Audrey's life. Then groups of ten at a time were taken into an adjoining room where they could see little Audrey through a large window.

While Vanessa and Debbie went in to see Audrey, I went to the chapel. It looked nearly the same as when I had visited there the previous December with Gina and Harriet. A little cup containing a small wooden crucifix was filled with about a quarter inch of oil. A statue of the Blessed Virgin Mary was covered with oil as was the plate glass on which it stood.

The weather was beautiful. The sun was out and the temperature was in the sixties. Mass was held outside in the Santos' backyard. Two other priests and a bishop were present: Most Reverend Bishop Mauro Muldoon, O.F.M., Bishop of Juticalpa, Honduras, Father George Joyce, and Father Michael McNamara. The bishop was the main celebrant for the Mass that day.

The mysterious oil seemed to be everywhere. When it came time for Communion I noticed that there was oil on the paten. In fact, part of the oil clung to the sacred host I consumed. Then I noticed that there was oil mixed with the consecrated wine. I drank it and tasted the oil. I did not like the taste. I'm sure that my confreres on the altar experienced the same phenomena, but neither the bishop nor the other priests said anything.

After Mass we had benediction. We all went into Audrey's room and got the four bloodstained hosts from the tabernacle. Each host was in a small reliquary and each reliquary was put into a large monstrance. Together, they made a most impressive sight. We carried them out to the people who were sitting under a makeshift canvass tent. Their faces were ecstatic – full of wonder and joy. Bishop Muldoon seemed delighted by everything. After the prayers, we blessed the people with the four hosts. This extraordinary blessing will probably never happen again. The present Bishop of Worcester, Most Reverend Daniel Reilly, has said that only one host and one monstrance at a time may be used to bless the people. History was being made that day and we were not aware of it.

After the ceremonies were over, the bishop and priests visited Linda Santo in the house. One of the volunteers called me into the chapel and asked me to say a few words for videotaping. I was a little surprised because I did not know that this was going to happen. Well, I just got into the spirit of the situation. First, I put my fingers on one of the small mirror plates on the edge of the altar where I was standing and I showed how the oil came off on my fingers. Then I began talking about the oil that was present on the altar and especially the chalice that was sticky with oil. I described what I had experienced during Mass that very day.[15]

On one visit to little Audrey's, I unexpectedly bumped into the TV crew of the renowned talk show *20/20*. My brother Richard was my chauffeur that day. When we arrived at the church parking lot, one of the Santos came over and told us to get in his car. A gentleman slid in beside me and introduced himself as a reporter from *20/20*. He was there to see if what was going on at little Audrey's home was interesting enough to broadcast. Since it was a beautiful day, the Mass was said outside on the back porch. The reporter followed everything very carefully. I noticed that he paid a great deal of attention to Mary Cormier who usually gave an introductory talk to the pilgrims before she would invite Linda to come out and say a few words. The man happened to be Jewish. Mary told him that the rabbi's wife who lived across the street came in to visit with Linda on occasion. I guess the reporter was sufficiently impressed by what he saw that day because little Audrey was featured on *20/20* on November 24, 1998.

One good thing about having family in the South Boston area is that I have lots of built in reasons for heading east from time to time, and therefore lots of opportunities to take people along with me for visits to little Audrey's house.

One such occasion saw the arrival of Gene Robel, our pilgrimage leader from Chicago. We hooked up at the Holiday Inn at Logan Airport in Boston. Gene rented a car and we drove to Worcester. We stopped off for lunch and

---

[15] The videotape of this interview and that day's Mass is available at the Apostolate of a Silent Soul, 68 South Flagg Street, Worcester, Massachusetts, 01602.

then leisurely drove to Christ the King Church parking lot where one of the volunteers came to fetch us. Gene was ushered into the house and awaited his turn to go with a group of ten people to see little Audrey. They did not get into the room, but were able to see her through a window from an adjoining room. The volunteer then gave a brief history of Audrey's life. Afterwards we had Mass.

As I mentioned before, I always have something interesting happen to me whenever I go to see little Audrey. This time, the Boston-based TV show *Chronicles* had a crew there taping the goings on. Once again, I appeared on the altar at a Mass in the Santo home.

Gene Robel didn't make it on to the videotape, but his enthusiasm was undaunted nonetheless. He was so impressed with the weeping of oil in the chapel that he wanted to arrange a pilgrimage group from Chicago to see little Audrey. Consequently, Gene, Father Jim Holup, pastor of Assumption of the Blessed Virgin Mary in Ashkum, Illinois, and I left on February 30, 2000, with a group of about thirty-five people to Providence, Rhode Island. Another group of fourteen people were to arrive the next day. That Tuesday afternoon we had dinner and then Mass in the hotel. The next morning, we boarded a bus for our forty-minute trip to Worcester. Gene had brought with him a huge, life-like crucifix with real hair and red striped cuts across the body.

Knowing that every time I visit little Audrey something special happens, I was just wondering what it would be this time. I was not disappointed.

We arrived early and stopped off at Christ the King church parking lot. I took the group inside to see the church and the window that little Audrey is placed behind for her August 9 celebration every year. (Bishop Dan Reilly asked the family not to have the celebration in the Holy Cross Stadium which they had used on August 9, 1998.) One of the volunteers came to the parking lot and escorted us to the Santo home. We all entered the chapel where Mary Cormier gave a talk; Linda Santo then came out to say a few words.

I had previously invited Father George Joyce to meet us at the Santo home and was very happy to find him there when we arrived. Father Joyce and I share a special bond, having been side by side on the altar the day the host bled. I was anxious to see him again and relive that awesome moment. Moreover, all the people who traveled with Gene and I from Chicago wanted to see him as he had been the main celebrant that special day. He went into the chapel to say hello to the Chicago pilgrims and then returned to the living room where we spent some time together. Unfortunately, Father Joyce was not able to concelebrate Mass with me. He had been replaced as the spiritual director for the Apostolate of a Silent Soul. This position is now occupied by Father John Foley, pastor of Christ the King Church, the parish in which the Santos live. Melkite priest Father Charles McCarthy (no relation) has also been named "advisor." Father Joyce is retired now and lives in residence in his nephew's parish in the Diocese of Springfield, Massachusetts.

Several miraculous things happened while I celebrated Mass on that March 1, 2000. First of all, a picture of the Blessed Virgin Mary started to bleed oil; then, some of the people also saw the picture of Padre Pio bleeding oil. After Mass, Gene Robel left his large crucifix leaning against the altar. When we arrived the next day with the second group of pilgrims, Mary Cormier told us that Gene's crucifix had started bleeding oil during the night. (Ever since this event, Gene has committed himself to displaying this crucifix everywhere he can.) Then Linda mentioned that an empty ciborium, which she had placed beside the altar Wednesday morning, was found to be one-third filled with oil. She brought the ciborium into the dining room and placed it on the table where Father Jim Holup and I could see for ourselves.

On the bus trip back to the Providence airport, we were all filled with excitement at what we had witnessed that day. Everyone was repeating again and again all the wondrous events that had happened. My skin was covered with goose bumps. What a day! Some of the pilgrims were so moved that they wanted to come back with Gene and me on August 9 to see Audrey in person in the crying room window of Christ the King Church.

Why do I make these trips? First of all, because every time I'm near little Audrey, my spiritual life gets charged up again. Secondly, I've seen miracles happen in the lives of the people who visit little Audrey. It's my joy to share her with others, knowing what great things God will do through this meeting. As Gina says, "God is showing us these mysterious signs to touch the hearts of all those who witness them – to soften harden hearts, and to give encouragement and hope to the faithful."

New Wine, New Skins

The experience of the bleeding host continues to bear fruit in my life. It has transformed old associations and activities. Things that, perhaps, I had started taking for granted began wearing a different face, as if a new soul had entered into them.

A Blessing on the Knights of Columbus

My relationship with the Knights of Columbus began back in Las Vegas when I used to drive Father John Ryan to his Knights of Columbus meetings. He was at that time serving as chaplain for the Knights. Eventually, I myself joined the Msgr. Lamb Council there in Las Vegas and, later, the John Neuman Council in Morgan City, Louisiana.

One day in September 1992, while visiting one of our retirees in the intensive care unit of the hospital in Arlington Heights, I was approached by Bob McDermott. He had seen the Fourth Degree pin on my lapel. He then told me that the Holy Rosary Council there in Arlington Heights was looking for a chaplain. Would I be interested? I eventually attended one of the Knights' regular meetings where I was formerly asked by Grand Knight Joe Healy (1992-1993) if I would serve as chaplain. I was then nominated and unanimously chosen as chaplain for Holy Rosary Council Knights of Columbus #4483 of Arlington Heights, Illinois.

In 1996, I was also asked to be the Faithful Friar of the St. Elizabeth Ann Seton Fourth Degree Assembly 2410 in Arlington Heights.

Over the years, I have had ample opportunity to witness the work of the Knights of Columbus, particularly the Knights of the Arlington Heights Councils. They are outstanding in their commitment to helping their fellow man. Every year, Holy Rosary Council raises money to support the mentally challenged learning disabilities program located in the Arlington Heights area. They do so by means of their famous Tootsie Roll Drive. The Council also sponsors dinner/dance programs three times a year for the residents of the Clearbrook Center for the handicapped in Arlington Heights. The Knights and their families prepare a delicious sit-down supper and organize an evening of entertainment for all the handicapped and developmentally disabled members of the Clearbrook Center who can attend. In addition, the Council helps out seminarians by providing them with some pocket money.

As chaplain for the Knights, I am on hand to preside at Masses on their important feasts and celebrations. On Thanksgiving Day, I offer a special Mass for deceased members and their families. On Valentine's Day, I have been asked to offer a Mass in which members may renew their marriage vows. Each year I also preside at a Mass for the Women's Auxiliary of the Holy Rosary Council at which newly elected officers are installed.

Naturally, I also contribute a bit of violin playing at the annual St. Patrick's Day dinner/dance. The members, I am told, love the fact that they have an Irish fiddler priest among them.

Thanks to little Audrey and my experience of the bleeding host, my relationship with the Knights of Columbus took on a new dimension. During his tenure as head of the Holy Rosary Council, Past Grand Knight Thomas Lazarra (1996-1997) came up with the idea of holding a monthly rosary in keeping with the Council's name: Holy Rosary. Shortly after, Phil Krueger, who was later to become Grand Knight (1999-2000), volunteered to take over the organization of the monthly rosary on the second Tuesday of every month.

As chaplain, I wanted to help in this spiritual ministry. We started out with about 10 to 15 people, but interest really picked up after Phil invited a group of Hispanics from the neighboring suburbs to put on a play at the Knights of Columbus hall to tell the story of St. Juan Diego and the miraculous image of Our Lady of Guadalupe that appeared on his cloak. On another occasion, during Lent, Phil arranged for the late Father Rafael Orozco and a group from Santa Teresita Mission, Palatine, Illinois, to re-enact the passion and death of Jesus.

Other special rosary celebrations were held in May. Children of council members were invited to participate in the crowning of a statue of Our Blessed Mother. I was thrilled to see the number of faithful grow to as many as 120 on nights when these special programs were presented, especially since the rosary has held such a special place in my heart for so many years.

Then, in 1999, I began to bless the people with the oil from the Santo home. Right from the beginning, it was clear to me that the people loved to be blessed with this oil. I usually end our rosary night with a few words updating everyone on the life of little Audrey Santo and then give them a blessing with the oil. I discovered that by my witnessing and blessing I was directing people towards God. The results are there to see: the number of attendees for the Tuesday night rosary has escalated. How happy the Blessed Virgin Mary must be to see us all together!

Lay people may have never studied the theology of holy orders, but they understand nevertheless that we priests have a special relationship with God that allows us to stand in His place. They know that this is why they call us "Father." When I offer to bless people with the oil from little Audrey's home chapel, I can see the excitement in their eyes. They feel that God is touching them through me.

This is not to downplay the sacraments. The sacraments are the principle means by which God touches His people. But something as unique as the oil oozing from the religious figures in the Santo home can re-awaken the faithful and turn them toward the sacraments with even greater fervor. Touched by little Audrey's special oil, people feel special – like they have an "in" with their Father in Heaven.

My association with the Knights of Columbus has been long and mutually enriching. During a dinner honoring Past Grand Knight John Bauer, I realized just what my presence as a priest has meant to the Knights of the Arlington Heights area. At a certain moment during the evening, John stood up and said, "Can anyone guess what I have written in this envelope?"

Various people shouted out certain things like, "John Bauer, the next mayor of Arlington Heights!" and "John, I can't believe you actually won a jackpot on your last trip to

Las Vegas!" – the usual comments you hear at a roast of this kind.

Then John asked one of the ladies to open the envelope and read what he had written: "The greatest thing that I did as a Grand Knight for the Year 1995-96 was send Father Tom McCarthy to New Jersey to represent Holy Rosary Council during the Holy Father's visit to the United States." I was bowled over.

In 1999, along with Thad Steward, I was awarded the Faithful Navigators prestigious award at the annual Fourth Degree assembly held by Faithful Navigator Al Klein. Arlington Heights's *Daily Herald* reported:

> As chaplain of the Knights of Columbus in Arlington Heights, the Rev. Thomas McCarthy wears many hats. He does everything from playing lively jigs on his fiddle to leading the group in monthly Masses and the rosary. In fact, as their chaplain and an active member of the group's so-called "Fourth Degree," he could wear the fancy cape and feathered hat if he wanted to . . .

Regalia aside, the real honor is to be numbered among such extraordinary people.

A Musical Ministry

Through Gina Friend, I met Elaine Doerrfeld, an accomplished pianist, singer, teacher, and organist. Elaine was interested in the fact that I played violin downtown at the Irish Heritage Center in Chicago. During her years as a music teacher, Elaine had her classes go into the various nursing homes in the Algonquin, Illinois, area to hold sing-a-longs for the residents. She would organize the entertainment and play for the various programs. By the time I met her, however, her eyesight had begun to fail. Glaucoma made it difficult for her to see the notes on the page. She had to cut back on teaching, but she still had a great desire to share her God-given gifts with people.

Elaine invited me to come over and play some music with her. I said okay, but I made it clear I was no professional. I thought that maybe I could play well enough to accompany some sing-a-longs with her. Nothing too ambitious!

In the summer of 1998, Elaine and I prepared a half-hour program of Christmas music for the following holiday season. I have to say that I had to practice quite a bit in order to keep up with Elaine. She is a professional musician and a stickler for playing songs correctly. Also, Elaine wanted me to memorize our songs. I was glued to reading the music. I had to practice twice, even three times a day to come up to Elaine's expectations.

During the Christmas season that year, we played at five nursing homes in Elgin, Crystal Lake, and Niles. I didn't think I was that good, but Elaine was pleased with my playing. After Christmas, we whipped up an Irish music program, too. Our presentation is always the same: I introduce the song or medley by saying a little something about it, then we begin.

Our musical ministry has turned out to be a good way to bring the Lord's love to people. After Elaine and I are finished playing, I offer to bless the residents with the famous Irish blessing. The blessing is always very well received. It's a great satisfaction for me to see how the blessing comforts and raises the spirits of the elderly people we visit. On occasions, the directors have asked me to go into rooms to bless people who could not attend the sing-along because they are no longer ambulatory. Just to see their eyes light up when I come into the room gives me a joy beyond words. A little effort for so many smiles and happy faces. One lady, a Lutheran, asked me if a Lutheran could receive a blessing from a Catholic priest. Of course!

Several local newspapers have reported on this musical ministry. As part of their coverage, they include my experiences with little Audrey and the bleeding host. In this way, without even really trying, I have been able to widen my apostolate of witness to the Real Presence and bring little Audrey to the attention of even more people. The *Courier News* had this to say:

On a frigid Tuesday morning, Father Thomas McCarthy . . . could well have been sitting at home with his feet up. Instead, he was leading residents of Apostolic Christian Resthaven on Highland Avenue through a thirty-five minute seasonal sing-along . . . McCarthy, who was accompanied on piano by Elaine Doerrfeld of Algonquin, moved easily through the crowd and encouraged everyone to join in on the selected numbers . . .

While still in Boston, he became acquainted with Audrey Santo – a comatose young girl involved in a near drowning accident when she was a toddler. Things reported as miracles are said to have occurred around Audrey on more than one occasion . . . In addition, Audrey was once said to have had the stigmata, or blood stains similar to Christ's on the cross.

On a trip back east to visit Audrey in 1996, McCarthy encountered what he thinks was a miracle . . . A moment after the Communion host had been consecrated,

McCarthy looked down and saw a drop of blood on a smaller host . . .

After fifty years of saying Mass and more than 12,000 consecrations, McCarthy said the experience reaffirmed his priestly vocation.

He is by demeanor a rather deferential man, one not accustomed to the spotlight. Even in his musical presentation, McCarthy is more crowd cheerleader than center-stage player. He appears to deflect attention toward those in the house who are having the most fun in singing along. Thus, the recognition McCarthy has received since reportedly seeing the bleeding host has cast him more in the foreground than he is accustomed.

I'm a priest. Through me people touch God and are touched by God. That's my job. I know that both Elaine and I lift up these people with our music and our presence. But as a priest, I have the extra joy of physically touching the people with the sign of the cross that I put on their foreheads. The mysterious origin of the oils from the Santo home gives this ordinary priestly blessing another dimension. Mystery attracts people. It reminds them of God.

Family Healings

I mentioned in an earlier chapter that my brothers and sister and I are not very close. We love each other, and we are there for each other, but we have all taken different paths in life and, though we come together for the occasional reunion, we are not what I would call a "tight" family. Thanks to little Audrey, however, I have seen a closeness growing between my brothers and I that I would never have thought possible.

In October 1999, I returned to Boston to attend a family reunion commemorating the tenth anniversary of my mother's death. I asked my brother Richard to drive me out to little Audrey's since Ginny's asthma was particularly bad and she and Vincent had to stay home. Richard agreed to accompany me.

As usual, I said Mass in the Santo chapel. Afterwards, Linda allowed me to bring my brother in to see little Audrey. Suddenly, the lights flickered. My brother asked what was happening. The nurse explained that the lights dimmed whenever the air conditioner in the other room went on. Evidently the air conditioner was sapping the electricity for the monitor machines in little Audrey's room. It just so happens that my brother Richard is a first class electrician in the city of Boston. With a little nudging, I got him to offer to come out the next Monday to help put in a new electrical line to remedy the situation.

Richard enlisted the help of my brother Charlie and the two of them spent a whole day at the Santo home rewiring the air conditioner. At the end, Linda rewarded my brothers by letting them see little Audrey.

That evening, around 5:00 P.M., I was walking down the stairs of the rectory on my way to dinner with some friends. Lo and behold, my two brothers appeared around the corner. In another few minutes I would have missed them. I could see right away that something was up. Excitedly, Richard drew something out of his pocket. He held out his hand so I could see a pair of rosaries. "Tom, look! These are mother's rosaries that I kept after we buried her. See these rosaries . . . I put them into Little Audrey's hands and she clutched them . . . and her head seemed to move." Tears were streaming down his face. Evidently he had asked Linda's permission to do this, and she had said yes. "I asked little Audrey to bless my mother's rosaries. Her face just lit up like a Christmas tree and her whole upper body seemed to move with excitement."

My brother Richard has spent a lifetime working in construction as an electrician. He's worked in the cold and rain of many a terrible New England winter. He's not one to be very sensitive. But there he was, tears and all, sharing a moment of his life that he would never forget. As he spoke, my other brother Charlie was nodding his head up and down. I was amazed at what was transpiring between my two brothers. Both having children of their own, they were saddened by little Audrey's condition, particularly when Richard had difficulty getting mother's rosaries out of little Audrey's hands. Their hearts were melted by this little innocent, suffering one.

My brother Vincent had been trying for ages to get these two to make such a visit. Providence had lent a hand. Thanks to a few flickering lights, Richard and Charlie have also been touched by the wonder of little Audrey.

On another occasion, Richard and I were again at the Santo residence for the Wednesday Mass. This time, being a layman, he couldn't go in to see little Audrey, so he patiently waited while I made my visit. Then we went to the chapel for Mass.

As I was getting ready, I noticed that the chalice I was going to use on the altar was sticky with oil inside and outside of the cup. Even the paten was enrobed by a thick layer of oil. The Mass went on routinely – routinely for the Santo chapel, that is. I noticed that the Sacramentary cover was wet with oil and that some of the pages of the consecration prayers were also covered with oil. I wondered to myself why they didn't get a new book to replace this "dirty" volume and then remembered the oil was not there because of age and use. What would it serve to replace the book when another book would probably soon see the same results? Almost everything in the chapel is leaking oil. You can smell it all over the place. Afterwards, my brother told me that when I began to say Mass the statue of the Infant of Prague on the right side of the altar began to bleed oil right before his eyes. Phenomenal. Then, one of the volunteers brought over a twelve by twelve picture of the Blessed Virgin Mary and showed me were it was bleeding oil. You have to be there to appreciate the scale and power of these events.

After the Mass, I spent some time talking with Linda Santo and Mary Cormier, a former volunteer. Richard was busy talking with one of the pilgrims. When we left, we walked up Flagg Street towards our car. Suddenly my brother stopped and said to me, "Tom, take these rosaries." I took the rosaries from him. They were a bit warm, but I thought that this was because he had been holding them. Richard told me that after Mass a lady had come up to him and began talking about her illness and how she was in constant pain. She had come to see little Audrey to ask for a cure. My brother Richard, being a very kind person, talked and prayed with her. He wanted to do something for her. Then, on impulse, he said to the lady, "Here hold these rosaries. They will help heal you." When he put them into her hand she cried out, "These rosaries are burning my hand." My brother felt that, healing or no, some special grace had been received through the rosaries because of little Audrey's blessing. He now gladly drives me to say Mass at the Santo home and waits patiently as I visit little Audrey afterwards. He has become a firm believer in little Audrey as an instrument of God.

Still Going . . .

At present, I am not directly involved with little Audrey. If I were living in the vicinity, I would probably be over at the Santo home all the time. Being so far away, in Chicago, I am not able to be part of the every day goings on of the family. My role now is one of witness, particularly to prayer groups. I stay in touch with the Apostolate of a Silent Soul, and I keep people informed about what is happening around little Audrey. At least once a year I go myself to visit little Audrey, more often if Gene Robel and I are organizing a pilgrimage to Worcester. Gene has a lot of enthusiasm for such trips.

Gina Friend continues to open new roads for me. She has had me give my testimony on Catholic radio. She also sought out Jim Gilboy of CMJ publishers to do my autobiography. Jim and I met at the Palm Court Restaurant in Arlington Heights, destined once again to be the threshold of a new endeavor in my life. Jim told me that he felt there was something important in my story, something that people needed to hear. I walked away from the Palm Court Restaurant on cloud nine. God had made something of my life and now He was going to tell the whole world about it.

In the meantime, I continue to discover new ways to put my priesthood to work. Just recently, I joined a program offered by Golden Frontier Travel, a non-profit organization which arranges affordable tours to Catholic shrines in the United States and Canada. Golden Frontier tries to have a Catholic chaplain along for these tours to see to the spiritual needs of the pilgrims. So far this year, I have done four such bus tours. My first was a nine-day tour to upper Michigan. The second tour found me at the North American Martyrs shrine in Canada with time out for visits to see the famous Niagara Falls on the Canadian side. Then I did a nine-day trip to the North American Jesuit Martyrs shrine of Father Isaac Jogues and companions in Auriesville, New York – also the birthplace of Blessed Kateri Tekakwitha.

Last spring, our local paper in Arlington Heights, the *Daily Herald*, ran a story about my activities in the "Our Faith" section, complete with a picture of me in my bright green shirt – with Roman collar – playing fiddle at the Knights of Columbus in Arlington Heights. I don't think I had fully realized what a celebrity I had become until I read that article. I want to share this with you because it describes beautifully what God has done with my life since 1996. The article was the work of correspondent Eileen O. Daday:

> *He's an Irish priest from Boston who plays a mean jig on the fiddle and jams at the Irish American Heritage Center in Chicago. But here in the Northwest suburbs, the Rev. Thomas McCarthy also represents a connection to a highly publicized and unexplained series of religious events involving a comatose girl back in Boston. And because of that, this priest, who by all rights should be putting his feet up in retirement at Viatorian Retirement Center in Arlington Heights, is back in the thick of it.*
>
> *"Fans" of the unassuming 77-year-old priest arrange speaking engagements at local Catholic parishes, where he is eagerly greeted. His prayer sessions at the Knights of Columbus Hall in Arlington Heights, where he is chaplain, now draw at least a hundred people, said Phil Krueger, who organizes the prayer*

groups. "He's the best thing that ever happened to us," Krueger says.

. . . McCarthy became acquainted with the [Santo] family while serving in a parish in Boston and visits them occasionally when he goes back East. One visit he made to the home on June 5, 1996, changed his life. While there, he helped to celebrate a Mass with the Rev. George Joyce in the family chapel. After Joyce had consecrated the communion host, McCarthy looked down and saw blood appear on a smaller host.

"I couldn't believe it; I was amazed and didn't know what to think," McCarthy says. McCarthy was one of three priests on the altar. All three looked down in disbelief, and a gasp came from the thirty-five people in the chapel. "There was a presence you could feel in the room," McCarthy says.

If McCarthy had any doubts about how this event would change his life, it came immediately in the form of a microphone. The Libertyville-based Mercy Foundation happened to be filming a documentary about Audrey at the time. They filmed the Mass, caught the event on tape, and wanted his reaction. "I'm not sure if I would have believe it myself without it being on tape; I may have thought it was a vision," McCarthy says.

He concedes that after forty-eight years of saying Mass and more than 12,000 consecrations, it had become a daily habit. But witnessing what he believes was a miracle has resulted in a "deep reverence," and reaffirmed his priestly vocation.

His role in Audrey's developing story drew believers like Gina Friend of Wheeling, and Harriet Lechleider of Inverness to find him. They were driven to meet this humble priest who had witnessed what they took as God's presence. "I felt this very strong urge to meet him, and I couldn't believe he lived right here," Friend says. "I felt like I was meeting Moses. It's not that he has seen God, but he's a witness and he has a very special quality about him."

"God chooses very humble people to tell about miracles like this," Lechleider says. "He has a part in this; he should tell the story of what has happened there." With their prompting, he has spoken to prayer groups at St. Theresa Church in Palatine, Holy Family Church in Inverness, St. James Church in Arlington Heights, Mount St. Joseph in lake Zurich, Chapel of the Divine Word in Techny, and before the Mini-Marian Conference at the Odeum in Villa Park, in 1997.

. . . Most often it is people who have journeyed to Medjugorje who appeal to McCarthy to address their prayer groups. The result is he's finding himself more and more in demand. In some ways, it's a whole new vocation.

"Sometimes I don't feel worthy. I'd be more comfortable in the background," McCarthy says. "But I'm enjoying it; it's given me a whole new life."

A Priest Forever

Conclusion: A Love Letter

A wonderful thing happened to me on June 5, 1996. I came face to face with the living presence of Jesus the Son of the Most High God in a bleeding host. I witnessed a miraculous event that touched my heart and lifted up my soul and gave me a real incentive to go on living my priestly life.

I don't know why God chose me to receive this special grace. I am a simple priest. I am not a talented speaker like Billy Graham or a famous theologian like St. Augustine. I even need help preparing my homilies sometimes. My body long ago started its decline. I wear hearing aids and glasses. I worked hard all my life and went into retirement like everybody else. I play a little fiddle. I had to give up bowling and golf because of osteoarthritis. I'm really just an ordinary guy.

But whatever talents I have or don't have, it doesn't matter. The Lord chose me. Maybe that is just the point. Jesus wants people to know that the priesthood doesn't depend on human merit. It's a free gift from heaven. No matter how humble the individual priest may be, he is a source of life and salvation for God's people. Only the priest can bring God down to earth again in the form of the consecrated host and wine. This act is celebrated everyday, all over the world, by all kinds of priests, most of whom will never be famous. But the miracle is the same everywhere. Maybe God chose me, the smallest and simplest of his priestly band, so that people can see beyond the veil of the ordinary and routine and plunge into the mystery that is going on all the time before their eyes.

We priests acknowledge that every time we offer the Eucharist we are in the presence of Jesus the Son of the Living God. But to see the blood of a living body begin to flow from a consecrated host makes this daily act of faith an act of certitude. Thinking and writing about this now makes me tremble . . . somewhat fearful . . . filled with awe. Unfortunately, we fall into the routine of our priestly life. Just as married couples lose the early ardor of their honeymoon days as they sink into the monotony of every day life, we priests also can lose the wonder of who we are and what we are doing. As a Marriage Encounter priest, I have had to help people rediscover the bond that unites them. Little did I imagine that my Heavenly Father was going to find a way to help me rediscover the bond that unites me to Him and to His people!

When I try to explain to people the experience of the bleeding host, I often make the comparison to meeting a famous person. Just think how we all behave when we know the Holy Father is coming to visit. Imagine that you have been summoned for a personal meeting. Imagine facing the Pope eye to eye and feeling the touch of his hand. I remember how the crowd was thrilled by the Holy Father's presence in New Jersey a few years ago. I saw him arrive in a helicopter; he was some distance away from me, but I didn't care. I had seen the Pope in person!

But nothing can compare to the meeting I had on June 5, 1996. I use the word "meeting" because I want to convey what a personal encounter this was. It was not just an "event" or an "experience." It was a personal meeting between Jesus in the Eucharist and me. My God came to me in a private audience. How spectacular was that meeting! I can never forget it. Every time I lift up the host after the consecration, I wonder, will it bleed? I wonder because I know that the host is special, that it really is the body of Jesus. It can bleed like any other body. I know. I saw it happen.

By a singular grace of God I am dedicated to bringing you this good news. I didn't just happen to be in the right place at the right time on that June day in 1996. By God's Providence I was there. He wanted me to be a witness to this event. He wanted me to carry the word to thousands of people about his Real Presence in the Eucharist and in the souls of little silent ones like Audrey Santo. God sees what man cannot see. The prophet Samuel wanted to anoint each of Jesse's sons, but God did not choose any of them. David, the least likely in men's eyes, was God's man.

I know what the choice of God means. Many years ago, my Heavenly Father looked into my heart and saw that I loved Him. He was determined that I become a priest. He got me through every obstacle and accompanied me through fifty one years of priestly life. And just when I thought He was all finished with me, He called me again. Everything that has happened and is happening in my life from that day to this is a testament to the power of Jesus in my life.

Thank you, Lord, for this special blessing. Thank you, Jesus, for this wonderful experience of witnessing your real physical presence in my life. Thank you for choosing me from among the thousands of other Catholic priests in the United States to witness your bleeding host on the sacred altar of God in a humble one-car garage. Thank you for the gift of a new apostolate, a new family, a greater opportunity to give my all for you.

Do you think that you have nothing left to learn? If I thought that once, I do so no more. By nature, I like taking the back seat. I don't like to push myself forward. Yet, here I am learning to make public appearances, learning to be assertive and stand up and be heard. There's so much to do in this world to make it a better place, to bring comfort and consolation to others. We have to capitalize on our hidden talents. Even if you are fifty, sixty, seventy, or even eighty, you can still break free of that poor self-image that has dogged your steps for a lifetime. I did. I never thought that I would have the guts to go to a publisher and ask him to publish my autobiography. Amazing.

To all my brother priests out there reading this book, I want to tell you that you can do more than I can. You are more talented – I'm sure of it! Some of you are language scholars. How I wish I could master languages – but I've had to fight my way through Latin, Spanish, and French. Those of you who have this gift . . . give it to others freely. Teach English as a second language. Those of you who have musical talent, go out and lift up the hearts of the aged in nursing homes and hospitals. Sing with children. Draw them away from the television and video games. Those of you who can write, don't waste that gift because you don't think you are as good as Shakespeare. Write down your experiences as religious and priests and pass the wisdom of the spiritual life on to another generation. Help the laity understand our consecrated life by painting for them a picture in words.

Conclusion: A Love Letter

And finally, pastors, just a few words drawn from a half a century in the priesthood. Don't fail to take the opportunity to spend time with your people outside of presiding at ceremonies. Take that few minutes to walk across the bingo hall; stay after Mass and talk to your people; go to the receptions that follow a wedding or a funeral. Your people love you. They want to know you. They want to meet you. You don't have to have the personality of a movie star. Your presence alone does all the talking for you. It tells your people that you are available for them. I know so many prayer groups that meet in various churches and never see their parish priest. These are parishioners who really want to be led further in their relationship with Christ. The priest is the man with the consecration, formation, and education to guide them and feed their spiritual hunger.

Take every opportunity to bless your people. They love to be blessed. Why is it that people always turn out for the four big sacramental days: Ash Wednesday, Holy Thursday, Palm Sunday, and the Feast of St. Blase? I think it is because the priest touches them. That's what Jesus did, and His touch was a healing touch. Why do we wait for people to be dying to give them this touch? Priests can be so creative with their blessings. Why not invite people up at the end of Mass for a blessing on their birthday, the successful delivery of a baby, graduation, Mother's and Father's Days, etc. There are so many opportunities! Retired priests, this is a ministry you can really get into: Ask people, "Would you like a blessing?" You will be amazed how happy they are to have this contact, through you, with God.

My chief objective in this book is to tell the world, and especially my brother priests, that things are not over when you reach retirement age. Retirement is fiction. I am living proof that life begins at seventy-six. From the first meeting I had with Gina and Harriet in the Palm Court Restaurant up until this very hour, I have been living a new life, doing things I never thought possible, going places and meeting people I never dreamed of. As I'm heading for the door, they ask me, "Tom, where are you going now?" Like Willie Nelson, I just keep singing, "On the road again . . . doing things that I never have done before . . . I can't wait to get on the road again."

Am I tired? Sometimes. Admittedly, I have all the aches and pains of getting old. But I love my life. I wake up in the morning and I look forward to another day of doing something for the Lord and His people. I find energy for every day because of the love of who I am, what I'm doing, and what I'm discovering in others. I will keep going as long as the Lord gives me the strength to get out of bed every day. Life is not over until the Lord calls you! Don't kill yourself off in your own mind before your time. Live! The Pope says we are living in a "culture of death." Fight that culture by letting yourself be fully alive. Look at me. I'm in my eighties and the Lord is not finished with me yet.

He's not finished with you yet, either.

"You are a priest forever . . ."

Appendix I
Chronology of Fr. McCarthy's Life and Work

May 12, 1920	Born, Jamaica Plain, Boston, Massachusetts
1945-1949	Loyola University, Chicago, Illinois
1949	Graduated with Ph.B. in Philosophy
August 19, 1947	First vows taken with Viatorians
1949-1953	Catholic University, School of Theology
1952	Graduated with M.A. in Religious Education
October 1, 1952	Priestly Ordination, St. Gabriel Church, Washington, D.C.
1953-1959	Teacher at Alleman High School, Rock Island, Illinois
1959-1964	Teacher at Spalding Institute, Peoria, Illinois
1964-1973	Teacher at Bishop Gorman High School, Las Vegas, Nevada
1973-1976	Pastor of Our Lady of Wisdom Church, Reno, Nevada
1976-1977	Sabbatical year of study at the School of Applied Theology, Berkeley, California
1977-1979	Parochial Vicar of Holy Cross Church, Morgan City, Louisiana

1979-1982	Assistant Pastor at St. Viator Church, Chicago, Illinois
1982-1983	Clinical Pastoral Student, Chicago, Illinois
1983-1986	Chaplain at Sunrise Hospital, Las Vegas, Nevada
1986-1989	Assistant Pastor at Immaculate Conception Parish, Marlboro, Massachusetts
1989-1992	Assistant Pastor at Sts. Peter and Paul Church, South Boston, Massachusetts
1992-1994	Coordinator of Viatorian Retirement Center
1996-present	Resident in the Viatorian Retirement Center, Arlington Heights, Illinois
	Apostle for the Eucharist

Work with Worldwide Marriage Encounter

First Marriage Encounter weekend:

Sacramento, California 1974

Team Priest:

Reno, Nevada 1975-1976

Berkeley, California 1976-1977

Morgan City, Louisiana 1977-1979

Chicago, Illinois 1979-1983

Las Vegas, Nevada 1983-1986

Appendix I

Boston, Massachusetts 1986-1992

Chicago, Illinois 1992-present

Marriage Encounter Ecclesial Team Priest:

Las Vegas, Nevada 1984-1986

Boston, Massachusetts 1987-1988

Chicago, Illinois 1995-1996

Work with Retrouvaille Weekends

First Retrouvaille weekend:

Attleboro, Massachusetts 1988

Team Priest:

Boston, Massachusetts 1988-1992

Chicago, Illinois 1992-present

Work with Beginnings Experience Weekends

First Beginnings Experience weekend:

Houston, Texas 1980

Team Priest:

Chicago, Illinois 1981-1984; 1992-2004

Las Vegas, Nevada 1984-1987

Appendix II

Publications by Father Thomas McCarthy, C.S.V.

Guide to the Catholic Sisterhoods in the United States
Catholic University of America Press
Washington, D.C.: Five editions: 1952-1964

Guide to the Diocesan Priesthood
Catholic University of America Press
Washington, D.C.: 1956

Dedication for the Laity
Daughters of St. Paul, Boston, MA: 1964

Editorial Consultant for "Religious Communities of Men and
Women" in *Encyclopedia for Home and School*
McGraw Hill: 1965

Challenge for Now
Western Printing Company
Reno, Nevada: 1974

*Priesthood and Brotherhood – 1978 Directory of Vocations
for Men*
Forward by Warren Boudreaux, Bishop of Houma-
Thibodaux
Paulist Press: 1978

Appendix III
Letter of Bishop Daniel P. Reilly
Ordinary of the Diocese of Worcester
Concerning Audrey Santo

Diocese of Worcester
Office of the Bishop
49 Elm Street
Worcester, MA 01609

EMBARGOED UNTIL January 21, 1999 11:00am EDT
Statement by Most Rev. Daniel P. Reilly, Bishop of
Worcester

Over the past eleven years, many unexplainable circumstances have occurred around an innocent, bed-ridden girl named Audrey Santo. In cooperation with the family, I have asked a team of esteemed medical and theological professionals to review the situation to determine its possible impact, negative or positive, on the family and the Catholic faithful.

After a year of careful planning and evaluation, the commission has reported its preliminary finds to me. A summary of those findings is available to anyone who requests them, but I want to share some specific thoughts and concerns at this time as Bishop of the Diocese of Worcester.

The most striking evidence of the presence of God in the Santo home is seen in the dedication of the family to Audrey. Their constant respect for her dignity as a child of God is a poignant reminder that God touches our lives through the love and devotion of others.

There are inexplicable manifestations of oils and other substances emanating from religious objects in the Santo home. They are still under study. The purpose of the Church's investigation is not simply to become a promoter of claims of the miraculous. Rather, it is to review the theological foundations for such claims to assure that the faithful who follow them are not being misled.

In the case of Audrey herself, more study is needed from medical and other professionals regarding her level of awareness and her ability to communicate with the people around her. This is critical to the basis of the claim of her ability to intercede with God. In the meantime, I urge continued prayers <u>for</u> Audrey and her family. But praying <u>to</u> Audrey is not acceptable in Catholic teaching.

We are not yet able to confirm claims of miraculous events occurring at Audrey's home or as a result of a visit to Audrey, or from the oils associated with her. One need not make a personal visit to the Santo home. Indeed, continued demand for personal visitation poses the risk of compromising the family's ability to continue to offer excellent care to their daughter.

Further study has also been recommended and approved by me regarding the composition and source of the oils and other substances. In doing this, I want to underscore that any paranormal occurrences are not miraculous in and of themselves. The consistent practice of the Catholic Church has been not to use such occurrences as verifications of miraculous claims.

Finally, a more systematic study must be done before the Church can even begin to evaluate the concept of "victim soul," which has been applied to Audrey. We must proceed quite cautiously here, since this term is not commonly used by the Church except for Christ himself who became the victim for our sins and transgressions on the cross.

While further study is being conducted, please pray for Audrey, for her family and for all those seeking healing and hope. I also ask for prayers to assist us so that this continued investigation will strengthen our faith in God's divine mercy and love.

For More Information

On Eucharistic Miracles:

Eucharistic Miracles
Joan Carroll Cruz
Tan Books and Publishers, Inc.
P.O. Box 424
Rockford, Illinois 61105
Phone: (800) 437-5876
Email: tan@tanbooks.com
Website: http://www.tanbooks.com

On Little Audrey Santo:

In God's Hands: The Miraculous Story of Little Audrey Santo
Thomas W. Petrisko
St. Andrew's Productions
6111 Steubenville Pike
McKees Rocks, PA 15136
Phone: (412) 787-9735
Fax: (412) 787-5204

Apostolate of a Silent Soul, Inc.
68 South Flagg St.
Worcester, MA 01602
(The Apostolate issues a monthly newsletter on all matters pertaining to little Audrey. For appointments or to arrange tours, call 508-755-8712.)

Diocese of Worcester
49 Elm Street

Worcester, MA 01609
Phone: (508) 791-7171
Fax: (508) 753-7180

The official diocesan statement concerning Audrey Santo, as well as the first investigative report, can be found at the diocese's web site: http://www.worcesterdiocese.org.

Or, contact Ray Delisle at Rdelisle@worcesterdiocese.org for further information concerning Audrey Santo and the diocese.

Audrey's Life: Voice of a Silent Soul (Video)
The Mercy Foundation
P.O. Box 383
Mundelein, IL 60060
Phone: (847) 247-8170 / Fax: (847) 367-7831

Little Audrey has also been featured on:

Unsolved Mysteries
June 6, 1999

20/20
November 24, 1998

Chronicles (with Clint Conley)
Station WCVB, Boston
November 19, 1998

Newspaper/Magazine articles about little Audrey:

"Tears for Audrey"
By Gene Weingarten
The Washington Post

Sunday, July 19, 1998

"Mass to Honor 'Miracle' Girl"
By Joe Heaney
The Boston Herald
Friday, June 12, 1998

"Thousands of Believers Join Audrey"
The Boston Herald
Monday, August 10, 1998
http://www.boston.com/dailyglobe/globehtml/222/Believing
_in_the_blessedness_of_Aud.shtml

"Libertyville Producer Captures Hearts Worldwide with Story"
By Eileen O. Daday
Daily Herald
Arlington Heights, IL
Saturday, March 20, 1999

"'Angel's' Anniversary"
by Paul Sullivan
Boston Herald
Tuesday, August 10, 1999

On the Clerics of St. Viator and Louis Querbes:

Director of Vocations
Fr. Dan Nolan, C.S.V.
Clerics of St. Viator
Provincial Offices
1212 East Euclid Street
Arlington Heights, Illinois 60004
Phone: (847) 398-0685 / Fax: (847) 394-4507

Website: www.viatorians.com

Available on request is Viatorian Father George J. Auger's free and abridged translation of the biography *Louis Querbes* by Léo Bonneville, C.S.V.

On Worldwide Marriage Encounter:
See web page: http://www.wwme.org
Or call: 1-800-795-5683

On Retrouvaille (Troubled Marriage) Weekends:
See web page: http://www.retrouvaille.org
Or call: 1-800-470-2230

On Beginnings Experience Weekends:
Beginnings Experience International Ministry Center
1247-171st Place
Hammond, IN 46324
Phone: 219-989-8915
Fax: 219-989-8916
Email: imc@beimc.attmail.com